Being a School Governor in England

Acknowledgements

I would like to thank all the governors, clerks, teachers and schools that have assisted me throughout my service as a governor. I would particularly like to thank my governor readers for the drafts of the chapters for this book and their feedback and my husband for his patient proofreading and questioning, which has helped me to hone the text.

To order our books please go to our website www.criticalpublishing.com or contact our distributor Ingram Publisher Services, telephone 01752 202301 or email IPSUK.orders@ingramcontent.com. Details of bulk order discounts can be found at www.criticalpublishing.com/delivery-information.

Our titles are also available in electronic format: for individual use via our website and for libraries and other institutions from all the major ebook platforms.

Being a School Governor in England

All You Need to Know

Mary Briggs

First published in 2023 by Critical Publishing Ltd

All rights reserved. No part of this publication may be reproduced, stored in a retrieval system, or transmitted in any form or by any means, electronic, mechanical, photocopying, recording or otherwise, without prior permission in writing from the publisher.

The authors have made every effort to ensure the accuracy of information contained in this publication, but assume no responsibility for any errors, inaccuracies, inconsistencies and omissions. Likewise, every effort has been made to contact copyright holders. If any copyright material has been reproduced unwittingly and without permission the Publisher will gladly receive information enabling them to rectify any error or omission in subsequent editions.

Copyright © 2023 Mary Briggs

British Library Cataloguing in Publication Data
A CIP record for this book is available from the British Library

ISBN: 978-1-915080-92-9

This book is also available in the following e-book formats:
EPUB ISBN: 978-1-915080-93-6
Adobe e-book ISBN: 978-1-915080-94-3

The right of Mary Briggs to be identified as the Author of this work has been asserted by her in accordance with the Copyright, Design and Patents Act 1988.

Text design by Greensplash
Cover design by Out of House Limited
Project management by Newgen Publishing UK
Printed and bound in Great Britain by 4edge, Essex

Critical Publishing
3 Connaught Road
St Albans
AL3 5RX

www.criticalpublishing.com

Printed on FSC accredited paper

CONTENTS

Meet the author	vi
Introduction	1
Chapter 1: Governance	3
Chapter 2: School governors	21
Chapter 3: External governors	33
Chapter 4: Specific roles on the governing body	45
Chapter 5: Governors' meetings	83
Chapter 6: Governors' role in monitoring	101
Chapter 7: School governors and controlling bodies	123
Chapter 8: Governance and inspections	133
Chapter 9: Further support	157
Glossary of useful terms	165
Index	179

Meet the author

Mary Briggs

I worked at Oxford Brookes University from 2013 until my retirement in 2022 as a Principal Lecturer and Programme Lead in Education.

My professional background is based in social care and teaching, both in special schools and mainstream schools as a teacher, deputy and headteacher in several different areas of the country. I have been involved in teaching and researching in three very different university settings. I am currently a governor at a primary and a secondary school and a trustee of a charity that works with educational settings. I have authored more than 20 books and numerous book chapters on educational topics.

Introduction

Welcome to this book about school governance in England. This text has been designed to support you if you are considering volunteering or have recently volunteered for the role of governor or trustee to ensure that you are fully informed before making your decision. It is also a useful book for anyone who has been a governor or trustee for a while and may benefit from reviewing specific aspects of the role. This book can be read from cover to cover or used as a reference to explore particular issues or seek advice and support. It includes a glossary of terms that governors and trustees from outside education can use as a reminder from time to time – like a lot of professions, education is full of jargon and acronyms. Looking at what these words or abbreviations stand for can help you develop a shared understanding and enable you to conduct your role more effectively.

The book is structured to provide you with an overview of what governance is, starting with Chapter 1, which looks at responsibilities and challenges. Chapter 2 explores the governor's roles from within the school and Chapter 3 explores those who do not work in school but still have an important part to play in governance. Chapter 4 looks more closely at specific roles that governors play in boards and committees and Chapter 5 continues this in-depth examination with a focus on meetings and the particular procedures. The role of governors in monitoring developments in school is dealt with in Chapter 6. The external organisations with which governors work form the content of Chapter 7 with some schools still under the local authority, some as stand-alone academies and others linked to multi-academy trusts, or MATs. Chapter 8 explores the relationship between governors' roles and the processes of inspections. The book concludes with Chapter 9, which indicates where further support and training are available from a variety of sources. There is also a glossary, which will help you to navigate the terminology and abbreviations.

2 INTRODUCTION

I have been a governor in one category or another for over 20 years, as well as being a trustee for a charity that has an educational element. I wish I'd had access to a text like this that could have helped me in the early years of my role, even though I had already been a professional in education for many years with an educational background. I hope that this book will provide you with a starting point, either to consider the role of governor or to continue to develop your existing role. I mention more than once that education is a rapidly changing sector, but what I have written here will continue to provide you with the key principles of governance, expectations of all parties and things to think about. The case studies are drawn from my experiences and are often an amalgam of several incidents. If you are a governor leader, you may find these useful as part of facilitating discussions with other governors to explore values and assumptions and develop a shared understanding of the full nature of governance. Being a governor is an interesting and worthwhile role and this book will support you with your decision to take it on and continue to develop your understanding and effectiveness.

Mary Briggs, 2023

Chapter 1
GOVERNANCE

Introduction

This chapter explores the role of governance in the school context. It discusses possible motivations for becoming a school governor and how they might influence your expectations of what the role can cover, particularly in relation to your values and views of the purposes of education. It also reviews an example of a code of conduct for governors that may impact your decision to become a governor. Alongside this you will read about the Nolan Principles (Committee on Standards in Public Life, 1995), which are the seven principles for public office that should guide the practice of governance in schools. The National Governance Association (NGA) (2023) offers guidance to all governors and produces templates for many of the procedures that governing bodies must address.

> **KEY IDEAS FOR EXPLORATION**
> - What is governance?
> - What do you think are the expectations of the role of governor?

What is governance?

You might associate the word 'governance' with governing, which can imply exercising control and making policies, particularly in relation to administration. School governance is not about control of a school but rather about offering the leaders of the school support and challenging them to conduct their roles appropriately. In doing this, a governing body looks at what has happened in the past and what is happening currently (the present). It also looks to the future of the organisation as a whole. The day-to-day business of running any school is the responsibility of the senior leadership team, which is often referred to as the operational side of the organisation. The overview of the school – which is the governors' remit – is focused on the strategic side.

Effective governance

Another way to consider what governance is involves thinking about how the effectiveness of governance can be judged. The Department for Education's (2020) *Governance Handbook* suggests three key areas of activity where the effectiveness can be evaluated.

- *Ensuring clarity of vision, ethos, and strategic direction.*
- *Holding executive leaders to account for the educational performance of the organisation and its pupils, and the effective and efficient performance management of staff; and*
- *Overseeing the financial performance of the organisation and making sure its money is well spent.*

(Department for Education, 2020, p 13)

Although this provides a broad overview, these are all linked through governors' in-depth knowledge of the school. You cannot tell whether monies are being employed effectively to support pupil achievement if you have no idea of the strategic priorities for the short, medium and long term across the age range of the school. There is a duty to consider how the school is delivering best value for the public money that funds education. The *Handbook* goes on to suggest that the three principal areas above can be divided into six features.

1. **Strategic** leadership that sets and champions vision, ethos, and strategy.
2. **Accountability** that drives up educational standards and financial performance.
3. **People** with the right skills, experience, qualities, and capacity.
4. **Structures** that reinforce clearly defined roles and responsibilities.
5. **Compliance** with statutory and contractual requirements.
6. **Evaluation** to monitor and improve the quality and impact of governance.

(Department for Education, 2020, p 13)

These aspects of effective governance are explored in greater detail in Chapter 6, which looks at monitoring procedures across a range of governance activities.

Terms of office

Governors usually serve for a fixed term of four years and are associated with a specific category of governor. At the end of the term, depending upon status, a governor may be asked whether they would like to serve another term. If, for example, you are a parent governor and your child/children have left the school, then you could be asked to serve on the governing body in a different capacity; however, without children at the school you could no longer stand as governor in the parent category. Governing bodies try to maintain a balance of new and more experienced governors to ensure continuity of support for the school. If everyone is new to the role, this can be challenging for both the governing body and the school while they develop an effective working relationship. Governing bodies usually comprise the headteacher/head of school, staff governors – both teaching and non-teaching – parent governors, community and local authority governors (the latter is only if the school is maintained by the local education authority); if it is an academy, then there are co-opted governors, while faith schools also have foundation governors. (These are discussed in greater detail in Chapters 2 and 3.)

Regulations came into effect on 1 September 2012 for governing bodies that wanted to reconstitute. The new regulations are the *School Governance (Constitution) (England) Regulations 2012* (UK Government, 2012).

The composition of governing bodies

The minimum number of governors in a voluntary-aided Catholic school, for example, is:

- at least two parent governors;
- the headteacher unless the headteacher resigns the office of governor according to the regulations;
- one staff governor;
- one local authority governor;
- sufficient foundation governors to ensure that they are in a majority of two over all other categories of governors combined.

The governing body may appoint such numbers of co-opted governors as they consider necessary. If the headteacher resigns as governor, the position cannot be taken by another member of staff as the headteacher may withdraw their resignation at any time by giving written notice to the clerk. The staff governor does not have to be a teacher. The local authority governor is nominated by the local authority but appointed by the governing body after having, in the opinion of the governing body, met any eligibility criteria it has set. There is no limit to co-opted governors, but they are still governors and if a governing body appoints co-opted governors it will have to have more foundation governors.

The process of becoming a governor

Anyone can be a governor if they are over 18 years of age, as no specific qualifications or skills are required at the start. You do need to anticipate the time commitment of between 10 and 20 days across the year, which is likely to include attending meetings and school visits – some of which will occur during normal school and working hours, while others will be scheduled in the evenings. Once you have made the decision that you would like to become a governor, unless a role on the governing body is part of your main work role within a school, there is usually an application process. An advertisement for a governor is triggered if there is a vacancy on a local body or committee. If more than one person applies for a vacancy, then there is a vote within that specific group – parents or teachers. For other categories of governor, an audit of the current body may have revealed a gap in experience/knowledge of an area such as finance; in this case, if you fit the requirements, you may be considered by the existing governors and/or the multi-academy trust governance. All governors are vetted under the Disclosing and Barring Service (DBS) as part of the safeguarding statutory requirements before being invited to attend a meeting and then asked whether they would like to join. Induction will include training in safeguarding and data safety, and possibly a course on health and safety. The mandatory area of training on an annual basis is safeguarding, as this is everyone's responsibility.

Code of conduct

The following is a description of a code of conduct, which is reviewed by the governors, signed annually and dated.

> *The governing body has adopted the following Code of Conduct based on the code developed by the National Governance Association (NGA). As individual members of the Local Governing Body we agree to the following:*

Role and responsibilities

These usually start with a general statement of the purpose of the governing body and the role of the headteacher, in particular that the governing body has an executive function, operating in all matters at a strategic level and leaving the executive head, headteacher/head of school and senior school leaders responsible and accountable for the operational day-to-day management of the school.

The main focus of any school is to ensure the educational achievement of all children/pupils/students. Also included in this introduction is the acceptance that the governing body normally acts as a whole rather than as individuals unless someone is given delegated authority to function as an individual on behalf of the governing body. Governors need to accept collective responsibility for all decisions made by the body or delegated individuals. In accepting this aspect of the process, governors will be expected not to talk against majority decisions outside the meetings. There are usually statements about acting fairly and without prejudice, and reviewing any decisions and their impacts on the school and its community. Governing bodies will expect governors and the school to promote tolerance and respect for people of all faiths (including those of no faith), cultures and lifestyles, and to provide support and help, through words, actions and influence, to prepare children and young people positively for life after school. There is also a statement about maintaining the ethos and reputation of the school while providing challenge to the school leadership.

After an introductory statement, the following areas may be explained in more detail.

Commitment

This includes the understanding that although governance requires the commitment of time and energy, it is balanced with the appreciation that governors are volunteers. Having said that there is a minimum expectation to be available to attend all meetings if possible, and to respond to communications as soon as possible. It will also be necessary to engage in necessary and appropriate training, including any associated with safeguarding and Keeping Children Safe in Education (KCSIE). Governors are expected to engage with school activities and visits to schools. Expectations of the number of visits are usually set out in this section. This would be worth exploring if you are interested in joining a governing body to assess whether you are able to meet the time commitment. This section may also include the disqualification of governors if they fail to engage over, say, a six-month period.

Attendance of governors is displayed on the governors' section of the school's website. Table 1.1 gives an example of this.

Table 1.1 Governing body information for the academic year (current year should appear on the school website)

Governor name	
Governor category	
Term of office starts	
Term of office ends	
Appointing body	
Committee membership	
Position of responsibility in the current year	
Attendance (This covers main governing body meetings and any sub committees.)	

Relationships

This section focuses on establishing good working relationships with other governors, school staff, pupils and parents. Part of this is responding to communications in a timely manner (between three and five working days). Governors agree to act appropriately in meetings and work within the protocols for any meetings.

Confidentiality

Governors agree to observe confidentiality where required for matters discussed and information received in the process of governance.

Communications

Governors are given a secure email address associated with the individual school and/or MAT to use in their role, rather than using a personal email. There are a number of reasons for this, including the confidentiality of all school-related information. Keeping personal and school emails separate can help you, as a governor, to keep your address books and contacts separate, reducing the chances of accidentally emailing confidential information to someone from outside the school. It also ensures that governors do not use email accounts they may share with family members as many households have shared computers and accounts. Although it is not mandated under General Data Protection Regulation (GDPR), using a specific email will help governors meet the requirement to prevent a data breach and then, if necessary, respond to subject access requests quickly. An additional advantage of using a school email is that it is often linked to a secure site where all school documents such as policies and governor papers are stored and can be accessed rather than having lots of hard copies of materials (see Chapter 5 for more details about governor meetings). If you are considering becoming a governor, it is worth reviewing your access to technology and how familiar you are with email and document repository sites. There is always help with getting things set up, including putting email systems on your phone that can reduce individual log-in processes and ensure you will receive information quickly. Accounts can also be linked to virtual meeting spaces as not all meetings may be held face to face, or a blended approach can be made available for those working away from home or where the combination of meeting time and travel make in-person attendance difficult.

Conflicts of interest

All governors must declare any pecuniary or other business interests (including those related to people with whom they are connected) in connection with the governing body's business in the Register of Business Interests, and if any such conflicted matter arises in a meeting it is necessary to offer to leave the meeting for the appropriate length of time. This requirement is updated every year; however, governors have a responsibility to declare any changes as soon as they occur.

This information is displayed on the governors' section of the school's website. Table 1.2 gives an example of this.

Table 1.2 Declaration of interests for the academic year (current year for the website)

Governor name	Name of organisation	Nature of business	Nature of interest	Governor at another school	Date declared

It is worth being aware that this information is in the public domain, thus offering a level of transparency about other organisations with which all governors are involved.

Breach of this code of conduct

As a governor signing up to a code of conduct, there is also an expectation that if any governor breaches this code, action will be taken. Usually the chair would investigate (unless the breach is committed by the chair, in which case it would be the vice-chair). If a resolution cannot be found, then a governor may be suspended or removed from their role, depending on the severity of the breach.

The code of conduct is then adopted by the governing body of this school, signed and dated.

Nolan Principles

Many schools/academies include the following principles explicitly in their code of conduct, while others use these and the areas suggested by the LGA to develop their own code of practice. You are able to see similarities in the expectations across a range of codes of conduct for every governing body or committee. These were introduced in 1995 by the UK Government Committee of Standards in Public Life (Committee on Standards in Public Life, 1995). They identify the important values enshrined in codes of conduct across the public sector, which includes education. Table 1.3 outlines the Nolan Principles.

Table 1.3 The seven principles of public life (adapted from Committee on Standards in Public Life, 1995)

	Principle	Definitions	What does this mean in practice?
1	Selflessness	Holders of public office should act solely in terms of the public interest.	
2	Integrity	Holders of public office must avoid placing themselves under any obligation to people or organisations that might try inappropriately to influence them in their work. They should not act or take decisions in order to gain financial or other material benefits for themselves, their family, or their friends. They must declare and resolve any interests and relationships.	

3	Objectivity	Holders of public office must act and take decisions impartially, fairly and on merit, using the best evidence and without discrimination or bias.	
4	Accountability	Holders of public office are accountable to the public for their decisions and actions and must submit themselves to the scrutiny necessary to ensure this.	
5	Openness	Holders of public office should act and take decisions in an open and transparent manner. Information should not be withheld from the public unless there are clear and lawful reasons for so doing.	
6	Honesty	Holders of public office should be truthful.	
7	Leadership	Holders of public office should exhibit these principles in their own behaviour and treat others with respect. They should actively promote and robustly support the principles and challenge poor behaviour wherever it occurs.	

> **THINGS TO CONSIDER**
>
> Read the code of conduct example and then review the Nolan Principles:
>
> - Complete the final column of Table 1.3 with examples of what you think the Nolan Principles mean in practice.
> - What do you notice about the key areas identified in both the code of conduct and the Nolan Principles?
> - Ask yourself: Can I make the commitment required to be a governor?
> - If you are thinking about volunteering or if you are already a governor, how easy is it to fit the commitment into the rest of your life?

Feedback

Your response to this task may vary depending on your experience. If you are a governor with several years' experience, then you may well be able to think of a range of examples in practice. However, if you are just beginning to consider applying to be a governor then don't worry if you are not able to think of specific examples. The case studies provided later in this chapter will help you think about the application of the Nolan Principles.

Motives for becoming a governor

People decide to become governors for quite varied reasons and you may have a clear agenda for your chosen role; however, it is important to recognise where your initial motivation may be in conflict with the actual role and the expectations required. For example, you may be a parent who feels they want to sort things out that are not going well for your child or children. You may be a teacher who is in opposition to the direction of travel of the school. In both cases, the individuals are thinking about governance as being operational rather than strategic, and they are looking for direct control. Both could become governors if they are aware of the responsibilities of governance and are clear about the roles they would be there to perform. (See Chapters 2 and 3 for a more detailed exploration of governors from within the school and those from outside.)

Some commercial and public services view their employees serving on a governing body as part of the whole organisation's community engagement, so will allow time during work to visit school and undertake governance duties. By law, employers must give employees who serve on maintained school boards *'reasonable time off'* to perform their duties under *Employment Rights Act 1996* (UK Government, 1996). The employee and employer must agree on what is *'reasonable time off'*. Employers may give time off with pay but are not required to do – this is a matter for discussion between the employee and the employer.

The following are two short case studies designed to illustrate the range of motives for becoming a governor and their potential implications.

CASE STUDY

A parent feels their child is not being stretched sufficiently with their learning in school. This is a critical issue for them and their family. They have also talked to other parents, who feel that more attention is given by the teachers to the children who are struggling than those who are more able. So their initial motive for joining the governors is to sort this issue out.

Feedback

Although asking questions about how the school meets the needs of all children is an appropriate and expected focus of discussions, it is not appropriate to discuss individual children at any meeting of governors. This goes against the idea of confidentiality from the code of conduct, even if the children you are discussing are your own. This approach would also bring into question a governor's objectivity – a governor needs to be able to stand back from their emotional connection to the issues and review the information they can assess. It can be easy to assume activities are or are not occurring in practice without access to the full evidence. (You may find it helpful at this point to turn to Chapter 6 about the governor's role in monitoring to see how governors can access the evidence upon which they can base questions about practice.) If you are a parent who is enthusiastic about your children's education, this is a great starting point; however, it must be tempered by keeping the discussion at a strategic level rather than straying into the operational and individualised levels. Discussions with other parents can be helpful, particularly as a parent governor; however, parents do need to discuss individual issues with the class or subject teacher in the first instance and not be drawn into discussing particular students' issues – especially if you are the parent.

> **THINGS TO CONSIDER**
>
> Governance is about asking questions for all children/students at the school, not for individuals, and as a governor you would need to be prepared to look at issues more generally and remain at the strategic level. Reflect on the following questions.
>
> - Can you put your personal issues aside as a governor?
> - Can you commit to finding out more about what goes on in classes and how would you plan to do this?
> - Are you prepared to look at the use of resources for all pupils and how might you go about doing this?

CASE STUDY

A local and active member of the community who ran support groups for young people showed interest in becoming a governor of their local school. Yet, while initially feeling they might have skills to offer, they were concerned about the level of financial knowledge required.

Feedback

Although there is a need to be able to ask questions about the finances of a school, as a governor there is no requirement for formal training in finance. Governing bodies conduct regular skills audits to ensure that there is a general and appropriate spread of skills and knowledge across all governors. A growing number of organisations also offer training for governors, including in the area of general finance and budgetary management. (Details of support and training can be found in Chapter 10.) If you are interested in becoming a governor, you can talk to existing members of the board of governors to find out more information ahead of making an application.

THINGS TO CONSIDER

- What might put you off thinking about becoming a governor?
- Can you commit to volunteering as a governor?
- Are you prepared to undertake training in order to up-skill?

> **WAYS OF WORKING**
>
> As a new governor, becoming familiar with the way that any governing body or committee works will take time. No one will expect you to be able to take on full duties until you have completed the induction process (see Chapter 9 for details of further support and training) and you will be able to work with a more experienced governor on monitoring activities (see Chapter 6 for aspects of monitoring). The goal of this chapter is to ensure that you have the necessary knowledge to make an informed decision about offering your services to a school in the role of governor.
>
> For the more experienced governor, this chapter acts as a reminder about the requirements of the role of governor and offers you an opportunity to reflect upon your involvement in the role to date. In addition, it may assist you in the recruitment of new governors.

References

Committee on Standards in Public Life (1995) *The Seven Principles of Public Life*. [online] Available at: www.gov.uk/government/publications/the-7-principles-of-public-life/the-7-principles-of-public-life--2 (accessed 8 March 2023).

Department for Education (2020) *Governance Handbook: Academy Trusts and Maintained Schools*. London: UK Government. [online] Available at: https://assets.publishing.service.gov.uk/government/uploads/system/uploads/attachment_data/file/925104/Governance_Handbook_FINAL.pdf (accessed 3 October 2022).

National Governance Association (NGA) (2022) Home page. [online] Available at: www.nga.org.uk/Home.aspx (accessed 3 October 2022).

UK Government (1996) *Employment Rights Act 1996*. [online] Available at: www.legislation.gov.uk/ukpga/1996/18/contents (accessed 3 October 2022).

UK Government (2012) *School Governance (Constitution) (England) Regulations*. [online] Available at: www.legislation.gov.uk/uksi/2012/1034 (accessed 3 October 2022).

Chapter 2
SCHOOL GOVERNORS

Introduction

This chapter introduces the role of governors who also work within the school. It examines the roles of the executive head, head of school/headteacher, teacher governor and non-teaching staff governor. School staff can sometimes feel that governors interfere with the day-to-day business of the school. Clearly, this is not their role; however, they are there to offer an outside perspective even if some of them do have knowledge and experience of education settings. School governors are there to induct non-school governors into the world of education. Every professional area develops its own jargon and uses abbreviations for activities that are familiar to those on the inside, but such language can be both misleading and confusing to those outside the profession. An important part of being a governor from inside the school is to understand that not everyone shares the same knowledge and experience of things as you do every day at work. If you are a teacher who has not engaged with governance, this chapter should allow you to see how you might get involved. If you are considering a governor's role from outside the school as a place of work, this chapter will help you to understand how various aspects of the school's day-to-day work are represented within a governing body or governance committee.

There are two different approaches to the constitution of governing bodies, depending on whether schools are maintained schools (under local authority control) or multi-academy trusts (MATs). Depending upon the status of the school you are considering joining, the governing body or committee will have slightly different composition.

Currently, for maintained schools, the document *Constitution of Governing Bodies of Maintained Schools* (Department for Education, 2017) details all the expected roles and responsibilities of governors. For multi-academy trusts, the document *Model Articles of Association for Academy Trusts* (Department for Education, 2021) is the reference for the details of the expected roles.

> **KEY IDEAS FOR EXPLORATION**
>
> - What are the differences and similarities in the roles of school governors?
> - What might be the expectations of behaviours as a school governor?
> - What do you need to understand about governance in order to take on the role as a governor?
> - What are the benefits for staff of becoming governors, either in their own school or elsewhere?

Executive head

Executive headteachers work across two or more schools, which may be under the control of the local authority, part of a free-standing academy of two or more schools or part of a MAT consisting of a number of different schools. They may attend all the governors' meetings, depending on time and workload. They will offer a view of a school in relation to the strategic vision for all the schools under their leadership. Sometimes, for governing bodies or committees, it can be difficult for the members to clearly see where the authority and responsibility lies for an individual school when the person at the top of the senior leadership is responsible for more than one school, which may also cover different age ranges. The executive head will need to be clear with their heads of school what the scheme of delegation is for each senior leader. Most often the executive head is responsible for leading the strategic direction of all the schools under their control; they will also be responsible for developing and appraising the heads of school. The heads of school are usually responsible for the day-to-day operational aspect of their school.

Headteacher

A teacher who is a headteacher is a governor because they hold this position in the school (unless they resign as a governor). If a teacher has the title headteacher, they are the person in charge of the school and are responsible for both leading the strategic direction of the school and the day-to-day operational side of the organisation. A headteacher would expect to meet with the chair of governors on a regular basis throughout the year to update them on everything that is happening in the school. This can be an opportunity as a teacher to use the chair as a sounding board for ideas. The chair would be expected to ask questions and both support and challenge through this process. (More information about the role of the chair can be found in Chapter 4.) The headteacher would also be responsible for providing a report ahead of each of the governing body meetings. Ideally, this would occur about a week before the meeting to give governors a chance to read carefully and come to the meeting with any questions and/or comments. A headteacher as a governor may vote on decisions within meetings unless they have resigned as a governor.

A secondary school report might have the following areas:

- operational update;
- staffing;
- staff well-being;

- self-evaluation (SEF)/update on school development plan (SDP) or school improvement plan (SIP) (depending upon the time of the year;
- behaviour for learning;
- Year 11 progress grades;
- Year 13 progress grades;
- attendance;
- safeguarding;
- pupil premium grant (PPG);
- exclusions;
- capital projects;
- risk register.

For a primary school, the areas would be similar – for example:

- strategy, vision and ethos;
- governance;
- compliance (including safeguarding, PPG, attendance and exclusions);
- stakeholder engagement and communication;
- education, curriculum and performance (including developments and data);
- report on progress on the school/academy development/ improvement plan (again depending upon the time of year this could be the self-evaluation stage of reviewing last year before setting objectives for the coming year, or it could be reviewing progress towards targets already set);
- staffing, HR and pay;
- operational management;
- financial management;
- pupil premium grant;
- capital projects;
- risk register.

Whatever the phase of education a school covers – nursery, primary or secondary – if the organisation is linked to a specific faith group, part of the report will cover this aspect of the ethos – for example if a school is associated with the Church of England, then the focus will be on Christian distinctiveness.

> **CASE STUDY**
>
> A new headteacher appointed to an existing governing body finds it difficult to begin to work with the governors, who they see as interfering with the plans they have for the school. They are getting on with the business of running the school and initially collaborating with governors is low on their list of priorities.

Feedback

Establishing an effective working relationship can be hard at the beginning for a new headteacher, and they may feel that the governors are working against them and their plans. However, governors are there to support and challenge by holding the headteacher to account. This is not about being combative, but rather involves asking probing questions about decisions to ensure that the school is getting value for money and that resources are supporting the progress and achievements of all the learners in the school. It would be helpful for a new headteacher to engage with governors right from the start in order to collaborate with them rather than setting up barriers to future working relationships. Time spent early on making these connections will benefit the headteacher and the school so everyone has a clear sense of where the organisation is heading.

A new headteacher is a significant event for any school, and governors may initially be concerned that the new leader is planning major changes that could result, for example, in teachers leaving. There may be a clear rationale for the need to change things quickly if a school has not been successful with their last Ofsted. However, an outstanding school with a new headteacher obviously needs a different approach. The new headteacher will want to take their own approaches to leadership without losing the most successful aspects of school practices. Making sure that any governing body is clear about your vision for the school as a headteacher, and that it has opportunities to ask questions about the direction of travel is an important part of embedding the new school leadership, regardless of the category of the school's last inspection. This allows the governors to work at the strategic level rather than the operational level, which is the headteacher's domain.

> **THINGS TO CONSIDER**
>
> - As a new headteacher, have I met all members of the governing body or committee?
> - Have I set up regular meetings with the chair?
> - How can I introduce my vision for the school and allow the governors to engage with this?
> - Have I established clear lines of communication?
> - Have I begun to work with the clerk to the governors?
> - Does the school have a full governing body, including a teacher and non-teaching governor?

Head of school

The head of school will be responsible for the operational side of managing and leading the school. They will feed into the discussion with an executive head and/or a chief executive officer (CEO) within a MAT regarding the strategic direction of the whole organisation, which includes the school for which they are responsible. The head of school may be asked by the executive head to prepare the headteacher's report for the governors as detailed above for the headteacher. The main difference between a headteacher and a head of school is the accountability links.

Teacher

Teachers can become governors in three separate ways: as a teacher in their own school; as a parent governor at their children's school; or as a governor at a different school. The last of these could be as a community, foundation or co-opt governor. If you are a teacher, schools invite expressions of interest to join the governing body as a teacher member; here, you must be under a contract of employment. If there is more than one person interested in the position, then there would be a vote by the teachers in the school, with the person who receives the most votes taking on the role. This process should be conducted by a ballot and not a show of hands in a meeting. If no candidate stands, then the vacancy remains until a teacher comes forward. It is important that teacher governors understand that their role will not be to represent staff, nor to stand alongside the headteacher or senior leadership in being held to account by the governing body, but rather to operate as part of the governing body to provide strategic leadership and to hold the headteacher or senior leadership to account. If you are considering this role, it is important to be clear about the expectations of the role and conduct, and to ensure that these are agreed upon up front.

CASE STUDY

A teacher in a school has sets their sights on becoming a headteacher or head of school and wants to join the governing body to find out more about how this works.

Feedback

Part of the decision about joining a governing body is whether or not a teacher joins the governors in the school in which they are employed or another local school where they can offer their knowledge and expertise – perhaps in relation to special educational needs and disability (SEND).

> **THINGS TO CONSIDER**
>
> - What will joining the governing body give me in relation to skills and knowledge for my future career?
> - Do I have the time to commit to this role?
> - Would I learn more from involvement in my own school's governing body or from involvement in the governing body of a different school?

Non-teaching governor

In order to ensure that all types of staff are represented at schools, non-teaching staff are encouraged to engage with governance through a member of their group being a governor of the school. This is important as they see the operational side of the organisation in a unique way that is different from teachers, and therefore they will ask different questions. Commitment to attending the meetings can be a challenge for this group of staff as often they work on a part-time basis; however, their input is vital to ensure a holistic view of the organisation and how it works. As with teaching staff, if more than one person expresses an interest in the role, a ballot must be held to decide who takes up the role. Again it is important that teacher governors understand that their role will not be to represent non-teaching staff, or to stand alongside the headteacher or senior leadership in being held to account by the governing body, but rather to operate as part of the governing body to provide strategic leadership and to hold the headteacher or senior leadership to account. If you are considering this role, it is advisable to be clear about the expectations of role and conduct, and to ensure that these are agreed up front. This is not a specific role that is identified for maintained schools in the guidance; in practice, though, most schools seek a non-teaching governor as part of the body.

CASE STUDY

A non-teaching member of staff wants to join the governors as they do not see proposed changes to working patterns of teaching assistants as the right way to go and want something done about it. They see the governors as being in charge of the school and therefore think decisions can be overturned.

Feedback

Unfortunately, this person has not understood the role of governance, which is to hold the headteacher and senior leadership of the school to account. Any decisions should be scrutinised for their value for money and for maximising the opportunities for the pupils' educational progress. As a governor, you can ask for items to be on the meeting agenda for discussion; however, these should not focus on individual staff or pupils.

THINGS TO CONSIDER

- What do you understand so far about the remit of becoming a governor?
- How could you be objective about areas for discussion at meetings?
- What more could you learn from involvement in the governing body?

Clerk

Although not necessarily employed directly by the school, the clerk is a key role in the process of governance in schools. Clerks may be employed through the local authority or by a MAT to undertake their duties for a governing body. Clerks are there to provide independent and expert guidance and advice to the governors on governance, constitutional and procedural matters. The clerk provides secretarial support for governors writing minutes, keeping copies of meetings, sending out agendas and keeping logs of training and all the required documents, such as the code of conduct, declaration of interests and correspondence.

Agendas are organised in conjunction with the chair and the headteacher, although many MATs have standing items that they expect to be on all full governing body agendas. Clerks undertake regular professional training to keep them up to date with changes in procedures. The clerk is also responsible for letting governors know when their term of office is ending. If they undertake additional training, they will also organise all the correspondence associated with exclusions, appeals and complaints. The clerk is not a governor, but provides a vital service for all governors within a school. While they do not vote on any decisions at meetings, they record the outcomes of votes in the minutes.

> **THINGS TO CONSIDER**
> - As a school governor, what expertise do you bring to the governing body?
> - What do you think you would gain from involvement in governance for your professional development?

WAYS OF WORKING

As a governor from within the school system, you will need to consider how you will work effectively with people from outside the organisation. Governors appointed as a result of their role within school offer the whole governing body or committee access to their knowledge of education, the school, the curriculum and the pupils (even though the last are not discussed by name) to the working of the board and its meetings. Being a governor can be helpful as continuing professional development for teachers and non-teaching staff and can also help with the evaluation of day-to-day decisions to ensure effective education is provided for all pupils in the school.

Taking time to make sure that everyone has a shared understanding of terms used – particularly abbreviations – is important, as all professions develop their own ways of talking about things that are familiar to people inside the organisation. This helps people from outside the setting to understand more about ways of working in schools. It is important to be patient with people who ask questions about things with which you are familiar because it is part of your everyday practice. It is easy for activities to become routine and completed often without really thinking as they have become automatic. Everyone has experience of education and school, and this has an impact on how education for others is seen. Understanding how these experiences influence how others think about schools can be helpful when it comes to informing other governors about the changes since they were a pupil.

Education, like many of the public services in England, is constantly changing – including methods of teaching,

→

adaptions to the curriculum and the impact of technology. It can be a challenge for teachers to keep up to date let alone for those outside the profession. On any governing body, there is likely to be a range of knowledge and experience of the world of education and acknowledging this and planning for this in any presentations, reports or other activities is helpful to building an effective working relationship across the governing body. The chair (see Chapter 4 for more details about this role) can help to facilitate the discussion between the professionals and those outside the institution.

References

Department for Education (2017) *Constitution of Governing Bodies of Maintained Schools.* [online] Available at: www.gov.uk/government/publications/constitution-of-governing-bodies-of-maintained-schools (accessed 8 March 2023).

Department for Education (2021) *Model Articles of Association for Academy Trusts.* [online] Available at: www.gov.uk/government/publications/academy-model-memorandum-and-articles-of-association (accessed 8 March 2023).

Chapter 3
EXTERNAL GOVERNORS

Introduction

This chapter introduces the variety of governors and associated parties who come into the role of governor at different levels in school organisations from outside the school. These people may have experience of working in education in different settings or they may come from completely different work and experience backgrounds. As with all other governors' roles, each person needs to be over 18 years of age and not a student of the organisation to which they are applying to be a governor. You may be invited to join a governing body as you are seen to have the experience, knowledge and skills that may be missing after the body has conducted an audit of its existing members to identify any gaps.

KEY IDEAS FOR EXPLORATION

- What are the differences and similarities in the roles of school governors from outside the school?
- What might be the expectations of an external school governor?
- Which category of governor fits most closely with your experiences?

Parent governor

A parent governor obviously needs to be someone who is a parent or carer of a child/student attending the school to be eligible for this category of governor. Politicians often see parents as consumers of the education system, and much is made of parent choice and power in manifestos. However, a parent governor has exactly the same responsibilities as any other governor for a school to hold the senior leadership to account. A parent governor may be able to ask pertinent questions about discussion areas of which they have direct experience, such as potential changes to the uniform or the start and finish of the school day. From this example, they can provide a parental view rather than being seen as representing the parents. They are often in a good position to pick up concerns from playground discussions that can be passed on to the headteacher. They can also suggest to parents that they talk to staff in the school first if issues arise rather than perhaps adding to discussions either face to face or on a social media group. Parent governors can remain in the post until their term of office ends or their children leave the school. In order to take up their post, they are subject to the same vetting procedures as all other governor roles.

CASE STUDY

A parent governor is picking their child up from school and is accosted by an irate parent who says their child has been bullied by a group of pupils, particularly on the transport to school. They go on to explain that this is why they are picking their child up today. They are obviously not happy about this additional task. They want something done about the bullying situation and are clearly expecting the parent governor to do this for them.

Feedback

Anyone who has had to deal with someone who is upset and angry over events will know that this can be a challenging situation to deal with; however, a response is expected. If you can calm the irate parent down and ask about what has occurred, this can be helpful. You will then need to advise them to contact the school staff directly. All schools have clear behaviour policies and a zero tolerance for bullying to keep all pupils safe. You may feel that it is helpful to offer to go with the parent, not to solve the problem yourself but to add moral support. In this situation, in your role as a parent governor, you are not in a position to act directly in relation to the events. You could suggest that you raise the issue of bullying and how this is dealt with at the next governors' meeting so there can be a more detailed scrutiny of the issues for the school as this is part of the process of holding the senior leadership to account.

> **THINGS TO CONSIDER**
>
> - What are your true motives for becoming a governor?
> - What do you think you could bring to the role of parent governor?
> - How would you explain to other parents that you are not in the role to make decisions for them?

Community/co-opted governor

Community or co-opted governors are drawn from the local community through advertising for volunteers to become governors. The process of vetting, as described in Chapter 1, has to take place before the person is inducted into the body, board or committee. The other way of seeking co-opted members is as the result of a skills audit of the current members and identification of any key gaps. Below are some the areas that are asked about in an audit of each member before compiling the results for the whole group.

- *Strategy.* This is a core function of any governance, setting the vision and working on the strategy leadership of the organisation. It covers previous governance experience, development of strategy and chairing experience.
- *Accountability.* This is about the necessary knowledge to hold the leadership to account. It covers knowledge of school funding, knowledge and experience of working with budgets, curriculum and appraisal processes.
- *Working as a team.* Governance is not about individual members but rather how the members work as a team – how to develop their own knowledge of governance and the ability to form effective working relationships.
- *Key interrelationships.* This is about the structures and procedures of governance – how governance functions and expectations of all roles and responsibilities.
- *Compliance.* This relates to understanding the legal responsibilities of governance, including pupil suspensions, exclusions, staff grievances, under-performance and how all of these are handled, as well as how to speak up if things are not done appropriately.
- *Equality, diversity, and inclusion.* Again, this involves understanding the legal obligations in relation to such matters as recruitment of staff. Here knowledge of the community served by any school is key, together with how representative the governing body of that community is, however diverse the community may be.
- *Self-evaluation.* This requires reflecting on past events to help identify where to go next. For both the governing body and individual members, it involves identifying the direction of travel and any support required to achieve the vision.

It is worth noting that with more schools becoming MATs, some functions such as finance are not part of the scheme of delegation to governing bodies or committees. The knowledge and skills requirements have shifted to trustee level in these organisations. As a result, co-opted members are potentially likely to be drawn from professional roles that could support pupils in different aspects of their development, such as business, police or social work.

Local authority governor

Schools maintained by local authorities (LA) have a category of governor whereby the person is proposed by the local authority. This can be drawn from among local politicians or local people who have volunteered for the role of governor through the local authority.

> **CASE STUDY**
>
> A local councillor joins the governing body of a local secondary school with a clear agenda of promoting a selective approach to secondary education. The councillor feels strongly that a selective approach to secondary education will raise standards especially for the most able students.

Feedback

Although a councillor may wish to influence decisions made about education in their local area, that is not the role of governance. Being a councillor on a governing body can bring knowledge of who a school should approach about local events or decisions such as planning, road closures, speed limits near schools or other related issues. Governing bodies welcome the knowledge of future plans for the local area that a governor who is also a councillor might bring to the group.

Sometimes the boundaries between spheres of influence can be blurred in local areas. An example of this is the case of a parish councillor who had received reports of children riding their bikes without lights. As a concerned citizen, the parish councillor contacted the police to ask them to visit the local primary school. There are a number of issues surrounding these events that illustrate a lack of knowledge about the most appropriate lines of communication to resolve this situation. The parish councillor perhaps should ask the people reporting to them to contact the school directly and to follow this up with their own communication with school. The headteacher will be able to talk to the children about the dangers of riding their bikes without lights if they attend the school as they should be the main port of call for this kind of thing rather than someone outside the governors or school asking the police to become directly involved. The school may ask for police or road safety officers to speak to the children at a later stage. It is understandable that boundaries become blurred if people feel that children's safeguarding and welfare is at risk, although in this case the actions may well make communications between the parish council and the school more difficult in the future.

THINGS TO CONSIDER

- Is the role of governance seen as an integral part of being a councillor in your local area? If so, what is the rationale for this?
- Consider if a local councillor would have the time to commit to becoming a governor and explain your view.
- What might be the benefits of becoming a community/co-opted governor?

Foundation governor

A foundation governor can be in that position as a direct result of the office that they hold (ex-officio) such as the local vicar or priest for a church school. The appointment of foundation governors is related to the preservation and development of the religious character of the school. For example, a Church of England school may have foundation governors appointed by the parochial parish council. Likewise for a Muslim faith school, leaders of the local mosque may put forward people to serve on the governing body. In a faith school, these governors are usually the largest group on any of the boards or committees. These governors will also take a lead in any of the faith-based inspections that are covered under section 48 inspections, which are usually conducted separately from the Ofsted inspections of schools by a faith-based team. (See Chapter 8 for further details of the full range of inspections for schools.)

> **CASE STUDY**
>
> A local church-goer is keen to become involved in the local school and seeks a nomination from the parochial parish council. Their nomination is approved by the school and all the checks are completed. They make their way to their first meeting and are surprised to find that there is nothing about the religious distinctiveness on the meeting's agenda. They try to raise this as a question but this appears to go unheard in the meeting.

Feedback

If the school has a particular religious character that should be protected, then the new governor is right to raise the issue. If their voice has gone unheard in this meeting in the first instance, they need to approach the chair and the headteacher to discuss the matter. Visiting the school to find out more about what is taking place in relation to collective worship and religious education would also give evidence for the next round of discussion. It is appropriate to call the leadership, in this case the head and chair of governors, to account for whether this is part of the remit of the school. A section 48 inspection would find the school wanting if there was no discussion of this area of their activity.

> **THINGS TO CONSIDER**
>
> - How could you listen carefully to what is said in order to collect appropriate evidence to question the strategic leadership?
> - What sorts of questions could you ask to help you understand the position of those involved?
> - How are you able to collect evidence through visits to the school?
> - What might you learn from reviewing the school's self-evaluation form (SEF) in relation to its religious distinctiveness?
> - How are you able to check the expectations of foundation governors regarding section 48 inspections?

Associate roles

This category of role can be used to appoint someone to a committee as a result of their specific skills or expertise. They can be appointed to serve on one or more committees and they can attend full governing body meetings, although without voting rights as they are not seen as a governor. They can be given voting rights if the governing body agrees about the committee on which they may sit. These roles are often for a limited period or for a specific project.

Partnership governor

This category of governor is only required for foundation schools and special schools that do not have a foundation.

The governing body would seek nominations from appropriate religious organisations if the school were considered to have a religious character. Otherwise, parents or people within the community could suggest suitable candidates. Importantly, those nominated must be able to contribute to effective governance. They cannot be parents of current pupils, school staff or local authority employees involved in education. As with all other categories of governor, they are there to hold the leadership of the school to account rather than representing a specific interest group.

Trustees, members and directors

In MATs, different roles exist for people to be involved in governance (see Figure 3.1). Instead of the local authority having overall responsibility for a school or schools, the trust takes on that responsibility. Trustees are appointed to the board of the MAT and the vast majority of these are volunteers. Paying anyone in governance roles is subject to legal restrictions (Department for Education, 2020, p 55). All academy trusts, as charitable companies, have both academy trustees and members.

Figure 3.1 An example structure of a MAT

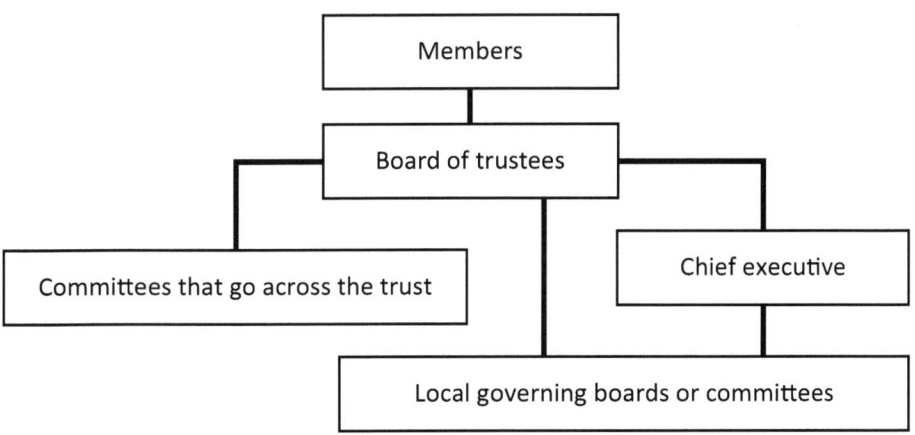

There should be a minimum of three members, although the preference is for there to be five. They:

- hold the responsibility as signatories of the articles of association at the outset of the MAT;
- can amend these articles of association as long as they do not contravene any of the regulations related to charities and/or the funding of the trust;
- appoint and remove trustees;
- direct trustees' actions;
- appoint auditors;
- have the power to dissolve the trust;
- cannot be employees of the trust.

For trustees the following guidelines apply.

- There must be at least two elected parents (though this can be at the local board level rather than trustee level in the MAT).
- Up to a third and no more can be employees of the academy trust.
- Up to 19.9 per cent and no more can be local authority, or have any commercial interest with the trustee up to four years previously.
- If the institution is a university technical college (UTC), the trustees must include a nominee from the sponsoring employer or university.

Members are in charge of the whole MAT and in most cases have a separate membership to the board of trustees.

See Chapter 7 for more detail about governance under different arrangements including schools as part of a MAT.

> **THINGS TO CONSIDER**
>
> - If you fit into several different categories of governor, which is the best one for you and why?

- Are you clear about the process of applying to become a governor? Note down the requirements to make sure.
- What skills and knowledge would you bring to the governors? Which area would you most like to develop your knowledge about?
- What time do you have available to commit to this role?

WAYS OF WORKING

Being a governor from outside the school can be a challenge as professional groups develop their own jargon, abbreviations and ways of describing things in a context where everyone shares the same meanings. For an outsider, following the thread of conversations while trying to remember what all the acronyms mean can prove difficult. Your role is to ask focused questions, and to do so you need to know exactly what is being discussed. Don't be afraid of asking for clarification about terms so you are clear about the discussion items in meetings and/or visits.

Reference

Department for Education (2020) *Governance Handbook: Academy Trusts and Maintained Schools.* [online] Available at: https://assets.publishing.service.gov.uk/government/uploads/system/uploads/attachment_data/file/925104/Governance_Handbook_FINAL.pdf (accessed 3 October 2022).

Chapter 4

SPECIFIC ROLES ON THE GOVERNING BODY

Introduction

This chapter provides more detail about specific roles on the governing body, and the expectations and responsibilities of these roles. It also begins to explore in more detail ways of monitoring within the roles discussed.

> **KEY IDEAS FOR EXPLORATION**
> - Taking on any of these specific roles comes with additional responsibilities.
> - Each of these roles also comes with the expectation of specific tasks such as visits to remain up to date with events in schools and to monitor activities in these areas.

Chair

The chair is an elected position from within the governors, although it is not held by a member of the teaching staff or anyone employed by the school or trust. In Catholic-maintained schools or trusts, it is usual practice to exclude anyone who is not a foundation governor from the office of chair. This practice is not seen in Church of England governing bodies or committees. The term of office varies from an annual review to one every two or three years. The chair is responsible for chairing meetings of the full governing board after setting the agenda with the senior leadership of the school and the clerk. (See Chapter 5 for details of the meetings, agenda, and items for discussion.) At these meetings, it is the chair's responsibility to ensure everyone gets an opportunity to speak as well as running the meeting to the agreed times. They also meet regularly with the headteacher to remain up to date with events at school and to act as a critical friend to the head. The chair should make sure everyone is involved in the governance process and roles are allocated equitably, taking account of individual strengths and the time each person has available for governance.

Key elements of the role include leading:

- application of appropriate governance;
- development of the governing team;
- the work with the school's senior leadership team;
- the improvement of the school;
- board/committee business.

Governance

The chair will set the ethos and the culture of the board/committee, drawing all members towards the values and goals of the organisation and its improvement. The chair should lead by example, making sure they have completed all the necessary training – especially the annual safeguarding updates. You will also need to ensure that you have read all the relevant papers for any meeting ahead of time and prepared some questions. You can model how you phrase these for others using open questions.

- Can you tell the board/committee about the comparison of a particular set of results with last year and how you see the trend in the data?

- There appears to be an increase in spending on alternative provision in this budget report. Could you tell us why this is the case?
- What is the school doing to recruit for the staff vacancies that you have reported?

These all provide an opportunity to explore items in headteacher reports or other papers in more detail. You are also modelling one method of holding the leadership to account. You can model how to offer support – for example, *'In your report, headteacher, it is pleasing to note the number of Year 13s who achieved their first choice of university place.'* Or, *'Perhaps it is worth drawing the board/committee's attention to the note from the local elderly care facility about how the children were received when they visited this month, their excellent behaviour impressed the residents and the staff.'*

For both of these examples, you would pass on thanks and congratulations to the staff and children/students involved, and want this recorded in the minutes as positive items and support for what the schools are doing for students' academic and personal development.

The chair will represent the full governors in appropriate meetings with LEA, MAT staff or other outside agencies, and correspond with these on matters where the governors can support the whole school and its community.

Leading and developing the governing team

Leading and developing any team can be challenging. In this context, all those with whom you will work are volunteers and therefore may not have a lot of time to give to the role. Talking to each of the members of the body or committee can be helpful in identifying their reasons for joining the governance of the school or MAT and their interests. Asking others to take on specific aspects of the governing functions should ideally involve matching their interests and the amount of time at their disposal to the tasks. This can mean that, as a chair, you pick up tasks that others are not keen to take on. Ideally, you will want to distribute the less-attractive roles across the group; however, this may not always be possible. Leading the team does not mean that you need or should do all the work yourself, although there can be a tendency for others to see this as a function of the chair. It is important to lead an audit of existing skills on the team so that there is a balance of knowledge and skills across the group. This process can be helpful if you wish to bring someone in with specific expertise as a co-opted or associate governor. (See Chapter 3 for more details about these types of governors.) Ultimately, developing the governing team means engaging with them, talking through how they see the role and ensuring there is a climate where others in the team can freely express their views and perspectives on how the team is working.

Working with the school's senior leadership team

Part of the chair's role is to engage in more frequent meetings with the leadership of the school or MAT between full governors' meetings. These are usually by mutual agreement and occur fortnightly or monthly, depending upon need. These meetings provide an opportunity for the chair to be kept up to date with all events in the school, ask questions and be a sounding board for ideas from the senior leadership team. Most chairs provide brief notes of these meetings for all other governors and report on meetings and any correspondence to the governing meetings. These are increasingly held electronically, with access given to all governors and, where appropriate, advisors, MAT central staff and inspectors.

The improvement plan

All schools will have a development or improvement plan that is developed following a review of the previous year and this will indicate the areas of focus for the current academic year. The main headings will be:

- quality of education;
- personal development;
- behaviour and attitudes;
- leadership and management.

These are the four main headings from the Ofsted inspection framework, but they allow individual schools in all age phases and MATs to concentrate on the key elements for driving improvements while allowing for contextual differences. The development/improvement plan will be discussed in each of the meetings with an expectation that the leadership team will report on progress and governors will provide comments and ask questions, led by the chair. (See Chapter 6 for more detail about how this document is used as part of the monitoring process undertaken by governors.)

Board/committee business

Part of the chair's role is managing the meetings. This means ensuring agendas are considered carefully to allow time to discuss appropriate items. (See Chapter 5 for a more detailed account of the agendas and meetings.) It also involves making sure everyone has an opportunity to speak and no single person monopolises the time available. Scanning the room is an important skill to ensure you have not missed anyone who would like to make a comment or ask a question. It is important to make sure the agenda for any meeting has been agreed with the head and clerk ahead of the date and that this and all papers are circulated to the whole body/committee at least a week ahead of the meeting date.

> **CASE STUDY**
>
> A parent governor wants to ask about the appropriateness of the spellings sent home for their child and raises this as an issue at a governing body meeting. They are concerned that more time is given to the children who have additional needs and insufficient time is given to those who are more able.
>
> - Consider how you might manage this as the chair. Which of the following would be the most appropriate strategy and why?
>   a. Allow the parent to continue discussing this topic.
>   b. Ask the parent whether they have spoken to the class teacher/form tutor and/or the headteacher and, if not, suggest they do speak to school staff.
>   c. Read the teaching and learning policy, check it is available for all on the school's website and ask questions about its implementation.
>   d. Suggest to the parent governor that raising personal concerns is always the right approach.
>   e. Suggest that inclusion and meeting the needs of all children/students should be the focus for a governor visit.
>   f. Talk to the class teacher/form tutor and ask them to sort this out.

Feedback

As a chair, you must realise that a parent's concerns are important to them; however, it is not an appropriate forum for discussion in the way it has been raised here. A focus on individual children is not a strategic oversight function for the governors, as this is operational. However, the question about how the school of whatever age phase meets the needs of all children is a critical issue for discussion as this may require a variety of resources and ways of working to enable all needs to be met. A brief explanation emphasising the main purpose of the meetings is helpful to set the scene as the starting point. Agree that monitoring meeting all children's/students' needs is a key role for governors and arrange for this to be part of the focus of forthcoming monitoring visits. You will want to talk to the parent governor outside the meeting to reassure them that they are being heard but also to let them know that their concerns need to be managed in a different way. Suggest they contact the class teacher/form tutor for a discussion in the first instance. If they are not happy with this, then the head of year or subject in secondary and headteacher in primary should be contacted to explore the issue further. It is not your role as chair to sort the issue out; rather, you should direct people to the right staff, who can address their issue.

THINGS TO CONSIDER

- If you are considering the role of chair, how would you make the time to be able to fulfil the requirements of the whole role?
- How could you bring the skills of agenda-setting and chairing meetings in other forums to the role?
- How do you think you work with others who could have different views from your own?
- Do you know where you could access training and/or future development opportunities for the role of chair? (See Chapter 10 for additional resources.)

Vice-chair

The vice-chair will stand in for the chair as and when required. Often this role is seen as the next chair in training, although this is not always the case. If you are considering standing as chair it can be useful to stand as vice-chair to gain a more detailed understanding of the role, expectations and responsibilities ahead of standing in the future. You will need to consider the increase in expectations of the time required between the role of vice-chair and chair before making a final decision.

> **THINGS TO CONSIDER**
>
> - If you are considering the role of vice-chair do you have the time to be able to fulfil the whole role?
> - What can you bring to the role of vice-chair that might complement the chair?
> - Do you know where you could access training and/or future development opportunities for the role of chair in the future? (See Chapter 10 for additional resources.)

Safeguarding governor

The role of safeguarding governor is probably one of the largest of the whole board or committee. As a result, it can only be held by a full governor – either elected or appointed – and it cannot be undertaken by an associate governor. Not only is it a complex area, but it underpins everything the school does. Although safeguarding is everyone's responsibility, the governor with this responsibility has a number of areas to monitor in detail. It is also a role that Ofsted is particularly focused on investigating during inspections.

This role is all about monitoring if there is an appropriate and ongoing culture of vigilance to keep children safe through the following aspects.

Ongoing staff and governor training in relation to safeguarding

Under the Keeping Children Safe in Education strategy (KCSIE) (Department for Education, 2022a), all staff and governors should receive up-to-date safeguarding training and have read the KCSIE document as well as the school's safeguarding/child protection policy (these are sometimes together in one document and sometimes separate). There should be a register of the completion of the training. Staff usually undertake their training as part of the training days at the beginning of the academic year in September. Governors should also complete their training around the same time, although some of their resources may be electronic rather than provided in face-to-face training sessions. Although one governor has the responsibility of monitoring safeguarding, everyone on the board/committee receives the training. Are there staff who are trained in the role of Designated Safeguarding Lead (DSL) ? Is their training updated regularly and is there always a DSL on the premises?

Physical environment: making sure all the checks have been conducted

Safeguarding the physical environment is important – for example, is the site closed to the public during the day or is there a right-of-way footpath across the outdoor area? Does the school share facilities with other organisations, a church, or a community centre or health centre? If so, are there shared entrances to the buildings? Inside the school, are there areas that provide hidden or semi-hidden spaces where bullying or child-on-child abuse could take place? If there are concerns about the physical environment, what measures are being put in place to mitigate these areas of risk?

A key place to check is visitor access to the school building. Look for the following:

- physical barriers or holding areas where identity can be checked;

- whether there is a sign-in process – either electronic or manual (some of the electronic sign-in systems take a picture of the person for the badge and for records when signing out);
- whether visitors are given information about safeguarding and who the DSL is if they need to report anything;
- whether there is safeguarding information on display on entry, including pictures of the DSL and team;
- whether visitors have signed to say they have received this information;
- whether visitors are given a badge or lanyard to identify them as a visitor around the school site.

Safer recruitment

In line with Part 3 of KCSIE (Department for Education, 2022a), governing bodies/MATs should ensure that they prevent people who pose a risk of harm from working with children through rigorous recruitment policies and procedures. Governors and MAT staff should make sure that there are written recruitment and selection policies and procedures in place. At least one panel member who conducts an interview should have completed safer recruitment training in line with the School Staffing (England) Regulations (UK Government, 2009).

Single central register

Table 4.1 below shows an example of a single central register (SCR), although as a safeguarding governor you are not expected to look at the completed register as this contains personal information about individuals. This may be the responsibility of the DSL or another senior leadership member of staff or an administrator, depending upon the size of the school. All original certificates and DBS clearances should be seen by those recruiting staff, volunteers or governors.

SPECIFIC ROLES ON THE GOVERNING BODY 55

Table 4.1 Example SCR

		N	O	T	S	T	A	T	U	T	O	R	Y
Volunteers only	Date of risk assessment completed												
Overseas checks	Checks completed yes/no												
	Checks required yes/no												
Right to work in the UK	Check evidenced date												
DBS certificate	Disclosure number	N	O	T	S	T	A	T	U	T	O	R	Y
	Original certificate seen												
Barred list check	Check evidenced date												
S128 Prohibited from management	Check evidenced date												
EEA list check	Check evidenced date												
GTCE list	Check evidenced date												
Prohibited list	Check evidenced date												
Qualifications	Check evidenced date												
	Required yes/no												
	Role												
	Start date												
Identity	Date evidence of ID seen												
	First name												
	Family name												

Notes on the sample register

The General Teaching Council England (GTCE) can confirm whether the teachers employed by a school, local authority or supply agency are fully registered.

All employers in England can use employer access to check the GTCE register and view details of a teacher's:

- qualified teacher status (QTS);
- induction record;
- disciplinary orders, if any exist;
- degree qualifications, where available.

The European Economic Area (EEA) was applied to checks if teachers had previously been employed in the European Union; however, since the withdrawal of the United Kingdom, these checks are no longer available. You may, however, see reference to this on older registers.

'S128 Prohibited from management' is a check to see if someone has been banned from management or governance of schools.

'Barred listing' is a check to see whether a person has been barred from working with children or young people.

Questions about the SCR

The following are some questions to ask specifically about the SCR as a safeguarding governor.

- How and where is the SCR stored? Is it secure?
- How frequently do you check the SCR?
- When is the last time you checked the SCR?
- Have you checked the information on the SCR for errors?
- Are all new staff recorded?
- Do you include supply teachers? If so, how long do they remain on the record?

- Are current volunteers for whom a DBS check has been conducted recorded?
- Are all relevant fields completed for each listed person?

Other aspects to monitor in relation to safeguarding

Table 4.2 shown on the next few pages presents some areas that are linked to safeguarding with an explanation of each aspect and some starter questions that you might explore with staff.

It can be worth identifying which areas you will look at each term to cover all aspects, although many will also be areas mentioned in the headteacher's report. You will also want to arrange discussions with the DSL in school to review ongoing issues at a strategic rather than an operational level.

To effectively fulfil the role of safeguarding governor, you should:

- have read the safeguarding and child protection policies;
- keep abreast of current safeguarding developments;
- try to attend in-service training sessions;
- meet regularly with the DSL;
- ask questions about safeguarding;
- make reports to the full governing body and/or appropriate committees regarding safeguarding oversight.

> **THINGS TO CONSIDER**
>
> - How could you manage your time effectively in the role of safeguarding governor?
> - Where could you access training and/or future development opportunities for the role of safeguarding governor? (See Chapter 10 for additional resources.)

Table 4.2 Areas linked to the safeguarding agenda

Aspects	What is this?	How can this be monitored?
Attendance	Those who do not attend school are more vulnerable, and this can be an early indication of safeguarding issues. For further guidance on recruitment, see Department for Education (2022b, 2022c).	What procedures are in place for checking the reasons for absence and how are these followed up by the school? Where there are safeguarding concerns, is there support through statutory children's social care?
Policies	Clear policies related to attendance, child protection, behaviour, safeguarding, staff conduct and whistleblowing are all relevant here, and should be in place and updated regularly.	What is the schedule of policy reviews? Are all relevant policies available to staff and parents?
Training	This is the training for safeguarding for all staff, governors, volunteers. It also includes safe recruitment training.	Is there a record of training attended and is non-attendance followed up?
Curriculum	There are opportunities in the curriculum to teach children/students about staying safe – for example, e-safety, but also the Sex and Relationships curriculum.	Can staff identify where in the curriculum children/students are explicitly taught about safeguarding themselves and others?

Induction	This mainly focuses on new staff at whatever level or role in the school. It should include relevant training and awareness of policies and practices.	Is there a record of the induction process for all new staff? How often is this reviewed in the light of new legislation?
Reflective supervision	This is a space for staff to reflect on their practice and critically evaluate experiences, as well as to debrief after challenging or stressful events. This is part of catering for staff well-being.	Are there opportunities for staff to talk to someone about safeguarding issues that might affect them as part of staff well-being?
Behaviour management	Part of behaviour management is how children and young people are expected to treat others, particularly in relation to child-on-child abuse.	Does the behaviour-management policy make clear links to safeguarding and child-on-child abuse? Are the preventions and consequences clear in the policy?
Safer recruitment	This is specific training around recruitment of staff working with children and young people. Further guidance on recruitment is available from Department for Education (2021).	Who are the staff trained? When was their training last updated? Are there written recruitment and selection policies and procedures in place?

↑

Table 4.2 (continued)

Aspects	What is this?	How can this be monitored?
E-safety	This is to ensure that children and young people are not groomed via the internet, making them vulnerable to a range of different forms of abuse.	It is worth asking questions about e-safety training, including what is taught about the use of electronic devices.
Staff and pupil well-being	This is linked to the reflective supervision element above. There might also be counselling available for children/students.	Are there different ways in which students can report their concerns about themselves, other children/students and or staff?
Children who are looked after (CLA) and SEND	Children/students in these categories are more vulnerable in relation to safeguarding and are 3.7 times more likely to be victims of abuse or neglect, so this needs to be factored into a strategic response to safeguarding.	It is worth asking questions about the overlap of safeguarding concerns reported and CLA and SEND children/students. Does the school notice any trends in the reporting? Are there activities in place specifically to support these groups?
School trips	School trips often take children/students away from the area they know. These need adequate staffing and preparatory visits in order to plan safe educational experiences for all children/students.	Are risk assessments clearly completed and logged for all trips? Are there adequate staffing levels for all trips?

Transitions	This can be taken in its widest form: transitions between lessons, transitions between schools, transitions between home and school.	How is information shared if children are transitioning between schools to ensure that key information is not lost in the process and children/students are kept safe? In secondary schools, transitions between classes can be a time when some students are more vulnerable to bullying – for example, how does the school prevent incidents from occurring?
On-call arrangements	This is a rota of staff who can be contacted outside school opening hours to ensure safeguarding – for example, where children/students are on residence trips.	Is there a rota of staff who can be contacted outside school hours? Is there cover if staff are on holiday?
Safeguarding context of the school	These are the factors around the home, community and location. It can be tempting to think that, for example, drugs are more common in urban areas when in fact rural poverty and other factors are impervious to the boundaries of areas of the country.	Discuss what the school know about contextual factors and how these might be mitigated for children and young people.

> **CASE STUDY**
>
> As a safeguarding governor, you notice that on a recent visit to the school the main entrance has been propped open as a delivery of materials is underway. However, there doesn't appear to be a member of staff visible. What risks have you witnessed?

Feedback

Although you can see that, when deliveries are being made, leaving the door open is convenient for the delivery person, this makes the building potentially vulnerable. If you saw this, you would need to report it as it represents a risk to the safety of the children/students.

> **THINGS TO CONSIDER**
>
> - Is there a clear protocol for deliveries into the building and is it clear who is responsible for their oversight?
> - Who is responsible for training/induction of the staff who should oversee this and when was this last conducted?
> - What actions will be taken by school staff after an incident like this is reported?

Special educational needs and disabilities governor

The special educational needs and disabilities (SEND) governor plays a vital role in ensuring that SEND stays on the governing body agenda and in providing a link between the governing body, any relevant committees and the staff with regard to special educational needs and disabilities.

This governor's duties include making every effort to see that the necessary special arrangements are made for pupils with special educational needs and disabilities. Asking questions about the training, advice and support available for all staff who are likely to teach these children/students is vital, to ensure they are aware of those needs and how they can best be met. This involves asking questions and consulting with the special educational needs co-ordinator (SENCo) about the current policy and practice in SEND and monitoring the progress and effectiveness of the governing body's policy on SEND, as well as monitoring the deployment of resources allocated to SEND and the effectiveness of communicating with parents.

To effectively fulfil the role of SEND governor, you will need to:

- have read the SEND policy document;
- keep abreast of current SEND developments;
- review your school's articulated vision for SEND learners;
- try to attend in-service training sessions;
- meet regularly with the SENCo;
- be clear about the school's expectations for SEND learners and how it intends to support them to achieve these;
- be aware of the progress SEND students are making in comparison with non-SEND students;
- ask questions about SEND and inclusion;
- make reports to the full governing body and/or appropriate committees regarding SEND oversight.

There are a number of practical ways whereby SEND governors can work with the chair and governing body in fulfilling its duties to provide appropriate support for children with special educational needs and disabilities. These may include:

- reviewing the school's vision, ethos and strategic direction for SEND learners;
- taking an active interest in the SEND register;

- taking part in school-based SEND training;
- being aware of parental views and concerns about SEND issues;
- providing encouragement for teachers and support assistants through discussions and visits to the school;
- being aware of changes to the code of practice and its impact on the school;
- checking that SEND is mentioned on the school improvement plan and reflected in the self-evaluation form (SEF);
- asking questions about staff training to support learner needs.

Specific questions you might ask

- How are SEND learners identified?
- What is the process once they are identified?
- What data are you recording to review this progress?
- What training are staff getting to support SEND learners?
- Which local agencies are you working with?

> **THINGS TO CONSIDER**
>
> - If you are considering the role of SEND governor, do you have the time to be able to fulfil the requirements of the entire role?
> - Do you know where you could access training and/or future development opportunities for the role of SEND governor? (See Chapter 10 for additional resources.)

PPG champion

The pupil premium grant (PPG) is a specific allocation of money to support disadvantaged groups of children/students, children of service families and children who are looked after. The following categories are eligible for the grant:

- children in year groups reception to Year 6 recorded as Ever 6 free school meals (FSM) as well as eligible children with no recourse to public funds (NRPF) in these year groups;
- students in Years 7 to 11 recorded as Ever 6 FSM as well as eligible NRPF pupils in these year groups;
- looked-after children (LAC), defined in the *Children Act 1989* (UK Government, 1989) as those who are in the care of, or provided with accommodation by, an English local authority;
- children who have ceased to be looked after by a local authority in England and Wales because of adoption, a special guardianship order or a child arrangements order (previously known as a residence order);
- children/students in year groups Reception to Year 11 recorded as Ever 6 service children or those in receipt of a child pension from the Ministry of Defence.

The PPG champion on a governing body should evaluate and monitor the impact of the use of the Pupil Premium/Catch Up Premium/PE and Sport Premium (as applicable) on children/students' progress and ensure that the funds are used to narrow the gap and improve outcomes. The use of these monies is reported separately, including details on the school's website.

A PPG champion should:

- receive term updates from the pupil premium lead;
- provide term updates to the appropriate subcommittees/full governing body meetings;
- invite the pupil premium lead to provide annual updates;
- undertake a school visit with the pupil premium lead;
- undertake relevant training;
- at least annually, contribute to a review of pupil premium statements and reports.

You should be reviewing how the monies have been spent on appropriate activities, which should include:

- supporting the quality of teaching, such as staff professional development;
- providing targeted academic support, such as tutoring;
- tackling non-academic barriers to success in school, such as attendance, behaviour, and social and emotional support.

E-safety governor

E-safety has become a much larger focus with the use of internet and social media as an arena where grooming of children/students takes place. It is therefore strongly linked to safeguarding processes. This can sometimes be seen as an integral part of linking with the subject of information communication technology (ICT) or computing, although because this is not about the wider taught curriculum in these areas, this is suggested as a separate role on a governing body.

The role of the e-safety governor involves overseeing five key areas:

1. managing, reviewing, promoting and evaluating the adherence to the online safety policy and strategy;
2. ensuring the right mechanisms are in place to support pupils, staff and parents facing online safety issues, including the designation of a safeguarding lead who is trained to support staff and consult with other agencies;
3. ensuring all staff receive appropriate online safety training that is relevant and that the training is refreshed annually;
4. measuring the effectiveness of child online safety education in the school, with the aim of delivering education that builds knowledge, skills and confidence;
5. educating parents and the whole school community about online safety.

This may seem to be a daunting list, yet you are not expected to do these things yourself as that is the operational side of the school's work. You are monitoring these areas to ensure they are in place and effective.

In order to become an effective e-safety governor, you will need to:

- understand governor responsibilities and accountabilities (Department for Education, 2022a);
- develop your awareness of online threats, risks and trends in technology and internet use in your school;
- support and critically challenge your school's implementation of online safety policies, procedures and practices;
- ask questions about the appropriate level of filtering and monitoring that safeguards young people from risky content and potential harmful contacts (consulting with the safeguarding governor and the DSL will be vital);
- receive regular online safety reports from the senior leadership team in school and again ask questions about the content;
- monitor to ensure all children/students are taught about online safeguarding as part of the whole curriculum;
- ask about the online safety training received by all staff.

Well-being governor

Especially since the COVID-19 pandemic, there has been a greater awareness of the impact of well-being and mental health on both children/students and staff in schools. The role of a well-being governor is to champion this area, ensuring that when decisions are made, the potential impact of well-being and mental health is thoroughly considered before final actions are taken.

As well as this, a governor focusing on this role will need to:

- ensure that the school gives thorough thought to how mental health and well-being can be embedded into the curriculum and other activities;
- ask for an audit of current provisions in order to develop any potential action plans for improvement;
- be ready to champion well-being and mental health at meetings and as part of any visits to the school.

If you took on the role of well-being governor, the following actions could be useful:

- learning walks around the school to see provision in practice and write reports for all governors;
- meetings with staff who have responsibility for well-being to discuss their plans and priorities for the coming months;
- student and staff voice surveys to measure the effectiveness of actions already taken;
- attending training sessions and webinars, and researching mental health in schools to ensure you are well informed to offer suggestions and monitor provision.

Foundation governor

A foundation governor most often has a role in representing a specific faith approach and the distinctiveness that brings to the ethos of the school. Christian distinctiveness is one example. For Catholic schools, foundation governors are appointed in the name of the bishop and have a legal duty to preserve and develop the Catholic character of the school/academy trust and to ensure that it is conducted in accordance with its trust deed. In Church of England schools, they are often nominated by the parochial parish council and agreed upon by the Diocesan Board of Education under which the school is based.

As a foundation governor, the kind of questions you might ask include the following.

- Why is the school doing this?
- Why is it doing it like this?
- Is this reflecting that the school is a church/faith school?
- How does this fit into the school development plan?
- Is the school being distinctively Christian (or distinctively related to the school's faith) in how it handles this?
- Are the school's principles and values shared and owned by the whole school community?
- Are the school's values inclusive?
- Do all members of the school community have a respect for faith and cultural diversity?
- Do the school's activities and displays encourage reflection?
- Is the school proud to be a church/faith school?

Foundation governors have a specific role to protect and develop the distinctive faith character of the school. This involves making sure the school is conducted in accordance with the trust deed, being a member of the governing body team and playing a full and active part. Foundation governors should also link between church and school or, where appropriate, the school and places of worship. In addition, they should initiate discussion on how the local church/place of worship can support its school. Their role also involves monitoring the impact of collective worship and religious education on children/students and staff, and supporting school leaders in preparing for and being part of the Statutory Inspection of Anglican/Methodist Schools (SIAMS) or section 48 inspections for other religious associated schools. (See Chapter 8 for more details about inspection procedures.)

As part of your role as a governor, you will be involved in monitoring what happens in schools. This might involve attending collective worship, visiting religious education lessons and meeting with children/students to talk to them about school.

Link governor

Most governing boards/committees have governors who are linked to specific curriculum subjects, such as mathematics or English, or they may be linked to careers, Sixth Form or almost any other area of activity inside or outside the school, depending on age phase.

As a link governor, you might undertake any of the following.

- Establish regular contact with person(s) within the school with responsibility for the governor's 'link' area. Ideally, this should occur once each term.
- Visit the school with a clear focus that has been agreed with the headteacher/subject leader prior to the visit. (See Chapter 6 for details of monitoring visits and other activities.)
- Support, encourage, challenge and provide a 'critical friend' role for the staff member with whom you are linked.
- Talk about resources to support the link area.
- Ask questions about how the link area caters for all learners – for example those with special educational needs and disability.
- Attend relevant training in school and for governors.
- Ensure you read all the policies related to the link area.
- Talk to students about their experience and opinions of the link area.
- Report to other governors about your findings from visits.

The role of link governor can be a good one to start with as a new governor, as it offers the opportunity to explore how the role works and at the same time explore an area of specific interest you might have as you enter governance.

Complaints, appeals, exclusions and pay committee

There are several other specific roles that governors can be asked to take on during their tenure. Many of these occur only when required or are annual events, such as the pay committee.

Sometimes all governors can be called to serve on these panels unless there are any conflicts of interest or they are employees of the school or trust. The first two panels discussed below are usually convened only when appropriate but for some governing bodies, the pay committee is an annual meeting.

Complaints and appeals

Complaints and appeals usually have three stages. The first stage is an investigation undertaken by the headteacher and the second stage is heard by a panel of governors. The governors' responsibility is to convene a panel of three impartial members with a clear remit of actions. No governor may sit on the panel if they have had a prior involvement in the complaint or in the circumstances surrounding it. In deciding the makeup of the panel, governors should try to ensure it is a cross-section of the categories of governor and there is a sensitivity to issues of race, gender and religious affiliation. On small governing bodies, the pool of people from whom the panel can be drawn can be restricted – especially when availability is taken into account. The clerk will usually arrange a meeting and the governors will hear the appeal or complaint, adhering to the procedures; these include identifying a member of the small team to chair the meeting and communicate the outcome to all parties.

More details about the procedures will be in the school/MAT appeals and complaints procedures, which will be available on the website and in any repository for policies documentation. These meetings are formally clerked, so there is a record of the proceedings. The final stage of appeal is to the Secretary of State for Education and complainants; the School Complaints Unit (SCU) will then examine whether the complaints policy and any other relevant policies were followed in accordance with the provisions set out. They will also examine policies to determine whether they adhere to education legislation. However, the department will not reinvestigate the substance of the complaint. If legislative or policy breaches are found, the SCU will report them to the school and the complainant and, where necessary, require remedial action to be taken.

Suspensions and exclusions

This can be a very challenging panel to be asked to serve on as it means hearing evidence about individual children/students and their families. The Department for Education sets out clear rules about the process of suspension and exclusions and the governors' role on this panel, which were updated in September 2022 (Department for Education, 2022d). According to this document, governing boards play an important role in ensuring that children who have been excluded from school receive a suitable education that facilitates their successful reintegration into education or meets their long-term needs. If a child/student is suspended, then work should be given by the school so their education continues. There should be a reintegration plan in place so that after a suspension, the child/student returns to school – sometimes in a staggered way, beginning with shorter periods in school and building up to returning full time.

For a permanent exclusions, governing boards have a key responsibility to consider whether excluded pupils should be reinstated. This forms part of their wider role to hold executive leaders to account for the lawful use of exclusion, in line with the duties set out in law, including equalities duties. This is undertaken by a panel of governors who must:

> *consider and decide on the reinstatement of a suspended or permanently excluded pupil within 15 school days of receiving notice of a suspension or permanent exclusion from the headteacher if:*
>
> - *it is a permanent exclusion;*
> - *it is a suspension which would bring the pupil's total number of school days out of school to more than 15 in a term; or*

- *it would result in the pupil missing a public examination or national curriculum test*

  (Department for Education, 2022d, p 34)

The clerk will invite:

- the child/student's parents, and automatically invite the student if they are 18 or over (for younger learners, parents can ask to bring the child/student to the meeting); the parent(s) are also informed that they can bring someone with them for support;
- relevant school staff, including the headteacher;
- a representative of the local authority if a maintained school;
- relevant staff from other agencies if they are involved with the child/student and their family.

All these groups will be asked to contribute to the meeting, sharing information from their perspective. The governors on the panel will ask questions after each of the representations from the parties. The meeting will be chaired by one of the governors, who will be responsible for managing the meeting, allowing for breaks where required and ensuring that all parties have time to communicate their arguments. The panel will then decide whether or not to uphold the headteacher's decision and then formally write to all parties to notify them of the final decision. If the decision is to uphold the exclusion, there is a right of appeal to the local authority.

CASE STUDY

On a panel hearing the case for an exclusion, one of the governors is concerned that the school has not understood the student's cultural heritage and has as a consequence responded negatively to the student's comments about the curriculum and attitude to school. The staff have seen this behaviour as an ongoing breach of the behaviour policy.

Feedback

Exclusions are a challenging part of a governor's role, as this is the last resort of any school's behaviour policy. Unfortunately, there is no evidence that students from particular groups are more likely than others to be excluded from school. These same groups of youngsters often suffer from racist abuse and/or bullying in schools. There can be issues around stereotyping of expected behaviours and sometimes marginalisation of students in these categories. The Timpson Report explored the data around this issue. It suggests that:

> *Schools must be places that are welcoming and respectful, where every child has the opportunity to succeed. To ensure this is the case, they should understand how their policies impact differently on pupils depending on their protected characteristics, such as disability or race, and should give particular consideration to the fair treatment of pupils from groups who are vulnerable to exclusion.*
>
> (Timpson, 2019, p 6)

Challenging though it might seem, the governor's role is to ask questions of the staff who have dealt with the young people about the measures they put in place to avoid exclusion. Did the school explore any SEND needs? Were considerations given to changes to the curriculum and timetable? Was an alternative provision considered as part of the package for this individual? One danger about issues related to specific groups is that it is seen as too difficult to address and people try to avoid possible confrontation and conflict; however, this is exactly why this does need to be addressed so appropriate changes can be made. Ultimately, after having reviewed all the evidence from all parties, the panel must make the decision to either uphold the exclusion or not.

> **THINGS TO CONSIDER**
>
> - What would you want to know about the role of a panel member before agreeing to take on this task?
> - How do you think you might feel about questioning the school's actions as part of a panel?

Pay committees

Pay committees are not an expected part of all governing bodies as many MATs have taken staffing and pay into the core functions of the organisation. If you are on a governing board/committee that does have this function, the expectation is that this panel will meet once a year after the round of appraisal meetings have taken place for all staff. The pay committee will be presented with the recommendation of pay awards for staff, with the list anonymised by the headteacher or senior leadership team. For teachers, this may mean an incremental increase in their salary or a double jump on the salary scale to reflect specific increases in responsibility and achievements in their role. It may also include notification of teachers moving from the initial main salary scale to the upper scale referred to as *'going through the threshold'*. This is the panel's opportunity to ask questions about the balance of experienced staff versus early career teachers, full-time and part-time contracts, and any potential risks there might be of losing staff in particular subjects at secondary level or in key roles at primary level. The pay committee may also be asked to look at the incremental awards for non-teaching staff.

Recruitment of staff

Governors do not undertake recruitment of staff independently. Within a local authority school, they will guide, support and manage the recruitment process – particularly for a headteacher. If the school is within a MAT, then they will take a lead on the whole recruitment process. Governors may be asked to join the discussion of person and job description prior to advertising, then shortlisting and the interview process, or at specific stages of the process. For other teaching staff, governors may or may not be asked to take part in the process. There is a personal and job specification to support this and these are translated into criteria for shortlisting and final selection. Sometimes governors are asked to undertake the safe recruitment training, although only one person on a panel is required to have completed this for the recruitment process to take place. Governors are not usually involved in the recruitment of other staff working in schools, such as teaching assistants, dinner supervisors, cover supervisors or office staff; however, trustees may be involved at MAT level.

> **CASE STUDY**
>
> On a recruitment panel, one of the governors says they want to appoint a male teacher as they feel he could control the students much better than a female teacher.

Feedback

The process of shortlisting and then interviewing leading to the offer of a post is structured around the job description and job specification (see Table 4.3).

SPECIFIC ROLES ON THE GOVERNING BODY 77

Table 4.3 An example of a shortlisting/interview grid for a class teacher

Scoring 3 = fully met; 2 = partially met; 1 = not met	Where assessed	Candidate 1	Candidate 2	Candidate 3
Recent experience of teaching in Year X (or surrounding year groups).	A, I			
Evidence of CPD and commitment to continuing further professional development.	A, I			
Working effectively as a member of a team. Developing good personal relationships within a team.	A, I, R			
Knowledge and experience of working with a range of professionals.	A, I			
Clear evidence of teaching consistently to a 'good' or 'outstanding' standard. Knowledge about planning creatively.	O, I			
Providing effectively for the individual needs of all children (eg classroom organisation and learning strategies).	O, I			

Table 4.3 (continued)

Scoring 3 = fully met; 2 = partially met; 1 = not met	Where assessed	Candidate 1	Candidate 2	Candidate 3
Demonstrating effective and accurate monitoring, assessment, recording and reporting of pupils' progress, including from last statutory assessment.	A, I			
Experience of working with pupils with additional needs.	A, I			
Knowledge of statutory requirements of legislation and own requirements to adhere to equal opportunities, health and safety, SEND and safeguarding.	A, I			
Promoting the school's aims positively, and use effective strategies to motivate and inspire the children.	A, I			
Establishing and developing close working relationships with parents, governors and the community.	A, I			

Creating a happy but challenging and effective learning environment, understanding the importance of a positive learning environment in promoting confident and independent learners.	I, O		
Effective organisational skills.	O, I		
Confident and competent user of ICT.	O, I		
Ability to promote excellent learning behaviours.	O, I		
Ability to communicate effectively with parents in order to develop support for children.	A, I		
Having high expectations of self and others.	A, I, O		
Approachable, enthusiastic, and motivational attitude.	I, O		
Total			

Key: A application, I interview, R references, O observed teaching session

From these are drawn up a range of criteria against each of the key elements. Each candidate is judged against exactly the same criteria to make the process as fair and equitable as possible. No process of this kind should relate to any of the protected characteristics under employment legislation and the *Equality Act 2010* (UK Government, 2010). These are: age; disability; gender reassignment; marriage and civil partnership; pregnancy and maternity; race, religion or belief; sex; and sexual orientation. While an individual may have a personal preference, the process of recruitment is to get the best person for the role, regardless of any pre-existing ideas that might be held. The role of the governors is to help find the right candidate to fill the vacancy using the most appropriate tools for the selection process.

> **THINGS TO CONSIDER**
>
> - What preconceived ideas do you have about the role of a teacher (if this is the role for which you are recruiting)?
> - What might be the personal challenges for you to consider if you were to be part of a recruitment team?

WAYS OF WORKING

In order to be an effective governor in any of the roles discussed above, you will need to:

- be clear about the role, expectations and responsibilities;
- take an active interest in the area;
- read the relevant policy documentation for the specific area of responsibility in detail;
- keep up to date with changes;
- try to attend training associated with your specific role;

- visit the school and meet with the key staff as regularly as possible;
- provide notes and updates for the full governing body if you have a specific role;
- be aware that there may be panels or committees that operate less frequently, which you may be asked to join.

References

Department for Education (2021) *Staffing and Employment Advice for Schools: Departmental Advice for School Leaders, Governing Bodies, Academy Trusts and Local Authorities*. London: UK Government. [online] Available at: https://assets.publishing.service.gov.uk/government/uploads/system/uploads/attachment_data/file/1026591/Staff_Advice_Handbook_Update_-_October_2021.pdf (accessed 12 November 2022).

Department for Education (2022a) *Keeping Children Safe in Education*. London: UK Government. [online] Available at: https://assets.publishing.service.gov.uk/government/uploads/system/uploads/attachment_data/file/1101454/Keeping_children_safe_in_education_2022.pdf (accessed 12 November 2022).

Department for Education (2022b) *Summary Table of Responsibilities for School Attendance: Guidance for Maintained Schools, Academies, Independent Schools, and Local Authorities*. London: UK Government. [online] Available at: https://assets.publishing.service.gov.uk/government/uploads/system/uploads/attachment_data/file/1073619/Summary_table_of_responsibilities_for_school_attendance.pdf (accessed 12 November 2022).

Department for Education (2022c) *Working Together to Improve School Attendance: Guidance for Maintained Schools, Academies, Independent Schools, and Local Authorities*. London: UK Government. [online] Available at: https://assets.publishing.service.gov.uk/government/uploads/system/uploads/attachment_data/file/1099677/Working_together_to_improve_school_attendance.pdf (accessed 12 November 2022).

Department for Education (2022d) *Suspension and Permanent Exclusion from Maintained Schools, Academies, and Pupil Referral Units in England, Including Pupil Movement Guidance for Maintained Schools, Academies, and Pupil Referral Units in England.* London: UK Government. [online] Available at: https://assets.publishing.service.gov.uk/government/uploads/system/uploads/attachment_data/file/1101498/Suspension_and_Permanent_Exclusion_from_maintained_schools__academies_and_pupil_referral_units_in_England__including_pupil_movement.pdf (accessed 12 November 2022).

Timpson, E (2019) *The Timpson Review of School Exclusion.* London: UK Government. [online] Available at: https://assets.publishing.service.gov.uk/government/uploads/system/uploads/attachment_data/file/807862/Timpson_review.pdf (accessed 19 November 2022).

UK Government (1989) *Children Act 1989.* [online] Available at: www.legislation.gov.uk/ukpga/1989/41/contents (accessed 14 March 2023).

UK Government (2009) *School Staffing (England) Regulations.* [online] Available at: www.legislation.gov.uk/uksi/2009/2680/contents/made (accessed 14 March 2023).

UK Government (2010) *Equality Act 2010.* [online] Available at: www.legislation.gov.uk/ukpga/2010/15/contents (accessed 21 November 2022).

Chapter 5
GOVERNORS' MEETINGS

Introduction

This chapter examines the format of governors' meetings and how these are conducted. You may be familiar with how meetings run at work or within clubs or committees, so much of the agenda and discussion of the items will be familiar to you already. What you may need to consider in more depth is the context and other governors' motivations for being involved. (See Chapter 1 for more detail about motives for becoming a governor.) Most meetings have a similar format and structure, so the items that appear regularly on agendas are there to ensure that statutory elements of the governing body's role are always covered.

> **KEY IDEAS FOR EXPLORATION**
>
> - What appears familiar to me as I read the agenda?
> - Which areas might I need to consider learning more about?
> - How do I prepare for my involvement in the meeting?
> - When is it appropriate to ask questions and how do I do that in this meeting?

Agenda

Table 5.1 is a sample agenda for a meeting with annotations to help you understand and interpret it.

Table 5.1 Sample governors' meeting agenda

No.	Item	Timings for items and who is leading on this – chair, clerk, headteacher, other staff or governors	Why are these on the agenda?	Additional notes
1	Welcome and opening prayer	Begins the meeting formally as soon as the time occurs on the agenda so an 18.30 start should indicate that is when everyone should be settled to begin.	Faith schools often start the meeting with a prayer as part of the welcome.	Opened by the chair unless the first meeting of the year before the chair is elected, when this is the clerk's role.
2	Apologies	From time to time members cannot attend but they do need to notify the clerk and the chair.	A record of governor attendance at meetings is kept and published on the school's website. When you join as a governor, there are clear expectations of attendance and governors can be asked to resign if they are not able to commit to being at meetings.	Clerk records this and it is also displayed on the school website.

3	Declaration of business interests	This is a statutory objection (see Nolan Principles discussed in Chapter 1).	As with other business meetings, there are expectations about declaring whether you work with the school or MAT in any capacity, whether you are related to staff and whether you work in a business that supplies services to the school/MAT.	Clerk keeps a record and so will the MAT.
4	Minutes of the last meeting dated	This is the formal record of the previous meeting. Support and challenge comments and questions are often identified by highlighting the minutes.	These are usually circulated a week before the meeting along with the agenda. The expectation is that participants will have read these and at this stage will either correct any inaccuracies and ask any specific questions that do not arise under the actions and matters arising.	These are usually voted on, proposed and seconded. They are then signed by the chair as a true record.

Table 5.1 (continued)

No.	Item	Timings for items and who is leading on this – chair, clerk, headteacher, other staff or governors	Why are these on the agenda?	Additional notes
5	Actions and matters arising	An important part of calling any member of the governors to account – have actions been completed on time?	These are often presented in a table at the end of the minutes and are 'RAG' rated: red for not completed, amber for partial and green for completed.	
6	Sub-committee minutes, if applicable (eg curriculum and standards, resources/finance, welfare and personal development	Minutes of the sub-committee are agreed as part of the individual sub-committee but always available to all members of the full governing body. Usually stored on a drive accessible to all and also presented as part of the full board meetings.	If a governing body is for a large secondary school and the scheme of delegation allows for it, there may be sub-committees. For smaller schools with different schemes of delegation from the MAT, there may be task and finish groups working on specific topics.	These are mainly for information unless questions have been raised prior to this meeting.

Governors' Meetings

7	Headteacher report	This can be a lengthy document that governors need time to review ahead of the meeting. As a governor, you will be looking at trends in data, subject areas where the attainment and progress have changed and increases in issues such as exclusions. For all of these, you would be expecting to ask questions about these patterns and what strategies the school/MAT is putting in place to address these.	This is usually a substantial report including **safeguarding, pupil premium, SEND, attendance, assessment data, if available, and staffing updates.** This should be with the governors at least a week before the meeting so they can read and formulate questions/queries/comments. The bold items are expected either as part of the report or reported separately on the agenda.	This is where the governors have a significant opportunity to ask questions about the information presented.

Table 5.1 (continued)

No.	Item	Timings for items and who is leading on this – chair, clerk, headteacher, other staff or governors	Why are these on the agenda?	Additional notes
8	SDP progress	This is developed from looking at all areas of the school to plan developments across all areas (see Chapter 6 for further details).	The school development plan or school improvement plan (SIP) should feature regularly on the agenda at meetings.	
9	Budget/finance		Depending on the scheme of delegation, this may be a report on the expenditure or it may be a discussion of funds for specific projects or budget-setting.	
10	Items for discussion, presentations		Sometimes these are shifted to an earlier slot of the agenda to allow staff to be	Presentations from a wider group of staff than the head and
11				
12				

				by teachers with a particular responsibility for a subject or area such as behaviour across the school		present who don't regularly attend the meetings so they can leave rather than staying for the whole meeting. Governors have a responsibility for staff welfare and this flexibility is part of that role.	senior leadership team offer governors a wider view of school practices alongside visits to the school.
13	Policies (circulated ahead of the meeting—sometimes to specific members of the governing body)	Governor responsibilities in relation to policies are discussed in Chapters 1 and 6.				MAT-wide policies often just require reading and acknowledging. Some school-specific policies may require a vote to accept them.	Schools and MATs should list their policies on the websites and there should also be a clear schedule for review. Some, such as safeguarding, are reviewed annually, while others have a longer shelf life unless there are changes in practices from government.

Table 5.1 (continued)

No.	Item	Timings for items and who is leading on this – chair, clerk, headteacher, other staff or governors	Why are these on the agenda?	Additional notes
14	Governor training	See further details in Chapter 10.	This includes training courses that are expected and further training opportunities. Annual declarations: KCSIE, governor effectiveness and skills audit.	
15	Items from the trust board	In some school-level agendas, this has been agreed to keep the channels of communication flowing and can be associated with a board-level representative attending meetings.	Depending on the scheme of delegation and the working relationships between the MAT and individual schools, this can vary from information to asking for school-level input to decision-making.	

GOVERNORS' MEETINGS

16	Matters of urgency – to be notified to clerk/chair/head 48 hours before the meeting	Sometimes still referred to as 'any other business' (AOB).
17	Items not for publication	This is not a regular item, but may include confidential information that is not appropriate to share more widely but about which governors need to be aware (eg headteacher's retirement).
18	Dates of next meeting	Dates for full governing bodies and any sub-committees are usually agreed at the beginning of the year to enable all those involved to plan their time.
19	End of meeting	This may include a closing prayer where church or other religious groups lead the school.

Specific roles within the meetings

- Agenda-setting is mainly the role of the clerk, head and chair, although all governors can ask for items to be included in the next meeting.
- Taking the minutes is the responsibility of the clerk, who can also advise the governors on procedures such as which items require a vote.
- Chairing/leading the discussion on items on the agenda is usually the chair, although they hand over to specific members of the teaching staff if they are presenting – for example, the headteacher's report by the head, head of department for a subject like mathematics, special needs coordinator to lead on SEND (SENCo), or a report on a specific issue by one of the governors. The other time the clerk chairs the meeting is at the beginning of the academic year, when the role of chair is agreed at the first meeting. Once agreed, the chair takes over the meeting. A good chair will try to balance giving everyone the opportunity to speak with moving through the agenda, which may mean closing the discussion on an item before everyone has finished. This may require coming back to this issue at a subsequent meeting or setting up a small group of governors to pursue this area further in between meetings. (See Chapter 4 on the chair for further details about this role.)

WAYS OF WORKING

The procedures in governors' meetings can vary depending on the relationships that have been established, although there should be a code of conduct requiring governors not to discuss confidential matters outside the meeting and how they should behave in the meeting. (See code of conduct in Chapter 1.) Although there may be variations in the levels of formality between governors in the meeting, they are a formal part of the governance of the school and as such generate a record that MATs and Ofsted scrutinise as part of the overview of governance. (See Chapter 7 for relationships with other controlling organisations and Chapter 8 for details about Ofsted inspections.) A good chair will be scanning the group to see whether anyone wishes to ask questions, usually by raising a hand. If several people want to speak, the chair may say, '*I will take questions from x, y and then z*'. in this way, they are signalling that all of these people have been seen as wanting to add comments or questions to the discussion and that they will be given the opportunity to speak in turn. Before the chair moves the meeting on, they may well ask whether there are any other comments or questions to complete the discussion on a specific item.

Preparation for governors' meetings

When you are attending meetings, it is important to prepare to engage with this specific activity. You should receive all the paperwork about a week ahead of the meeting. There is a caveat to this, however, as schools are complex and busy places, so sometimes material for some items may be received close to the meeting date or even tabled at the meeting. Depending on the item, the chair may ask the rest of the governing body whether the late materials should be rolled over to the next meeting to allow more time for reading and discussion. Education is an area where changes can take place quickly, and sometimes schools have little time to make changes. As a governor, you need to understand the situation in which teachers are working.

- Have you gained access to all the paperwork?
- Are you familiar with the key issues contained?
- Have you read the agenda and the minutes of the previous meeting?

- What specific themes and issues can you see in the minutes?
- Have you seen something that you would like to ask about – for example, a change in predicted exam results for a subject, a fall in attendance figures, a number of staff changes? It might be helpful to write your question down ahead of the meeting as it is easy to forget once the meeting starts.
- Do you know when and where the meeting will take place? (It is surprising how often this is overlooked, as schools can be busy places after teaching hours and parking may be an issue if large events are on at the same time as the meeting.)
- Do you know how to raise a question at the meeting? (There are differences in the way this is dealt with – often the meeting chair will have a preference for how this is approached.)
- Have you considered what kind of answer you are expecting to your question(s)?

CASE STUDY

A parent governor is concerned about bullying taking place in the school and has been approached by other parents to do something about what they see as a growing issue. The parent governor decides to raise this under 'any other business' at the next meeting and proceeds to lay down what they see should be done about this as the bullies appear not to be being punished, but instead are allowed to take part in recreational activities indoors while the rest of the children are out at playtime.

- Consider how you might handle this as the parent governor. Which of the following would be the most appropriate strategy?
    a. Demand action from the head and staff after the meeting.

> b. Ask the parents who approached you whether they have spoken to the class teacher/form tutor and/or the headteacher and, if not, suggest that they do speak to school staff.
> c. Read the behaviour policy, check that it is available for all parents on the school's website and ask questions about its implementation.
> d. Raise parental concerns as a parent governor under 'any other business'.
> e. Suggest that behaviour is a focus for a governors' visit.
> f. Talk to the class teacher/form tutor and ask them to sort this out.

Feedback

It can be difficult to manage such situations as a governor, as others see you as the person to 'sort thing out' whereas your role is in fact as a conduit for information. As a governor representing the parents, you should raise concerns – although ideally ahead of the meeting so this becomes an item for discussion. This rules out (d) as an appropriate strategy. Likewise, (f) is ruled out, as it is not your role to sort things out with individual teachers, as this would shift your role from strategic to operational – which is the headteacher's role. (See Chapter 1 for a discussion of what governance is.) Therefore, (b) and (c) are the first things to check, then a discussion should take place with the headteacher and chair about whether or not this should be an item for discussion at the next meeting in order to consider (e) as a means for the governors to obtain first-hand evidence of how behaviour is managed in the school.

THINGS TO CONSIDER

From this look at governors' meetings, you will need to consider the following points.

- Have you allowed sufficient time to prepare for the next governors' meeting to be fully engaged and effective as a governor?
- Are you clear about your role in the forthcoming meeting?
- Have you prepared your questions?
- Do you know the location and time of the meeting, and what time you need to arrive before the meeting starts?

Sub-committees

Sub-committees are usually smaller groups of governors who focus on a specific area such as resources or curriculum and standards. These committees can be more informal, although there are usually terms of reference for their scope.

An example of terms of reference

Curriculum and standards

The following issues are relevant.

- *Membership:* this indicates who sits on this committee.
- *Quorum:* in order for a meeting to proceed, there has to be an agreed number of governors present (this is the same for a full governing body).
- *Meetings:* this indicates the number of meetings held over the academic year.
- *Clerking:* this varies – large secondary schools often use a clerk for all meetings, whereas with small primary schools a member of the governing body may take the minutes of the meeting.

Guiding principles

The role of the curriculum committee is to advise the governing body about all matters relating to the curriculum, teaching and learning in the school, and to undertake certain responsibilities on behalf of the governing body.

To help it to perform its role and fulfil its purpose, the committee will draw up and implement a schedule of work each year. This schedule will help the committee to remain informed about the delivery of the curriculum and indicate how it will discharge its responsibilities.

Terms of reference

The committee has delegated to it the responsibility to:

- advise the Governing Body what targets should be set each year, and to assess and to report on the school's performance in pursuit of those targets;
- review annually and, where necessary, amend the school's curriculum policy statement to ensure it meets statutory requirements and promotes professional best practices;
- review at each meeting those aspects of the school development plan that relate to, or may have an impact on, the curriculum, teaching and learning;
- make the changes it thinks appropriate to those aspects of the plan for which it has responsibility;
- make any recommendations it thinks appropriate to other committees about the implications for the curriculum, teaching and learning of those aspects of the plan for which they are responsible;
- review annually the provision for children/students of all abilities to ensure the needs of all students are met, and to advise the governing body how provision may be improved;
- monitor the effectiveness of each of the following policies, formally reviewing each at least every three years and

approving them with such amendments as it considers appropriate – these will be listed below;
- review those aspects of any other school policies that relate to the curriculum, teaching and learning – for example, the equality policy – and, where necessary, to recommend either to the committee with responsibility for the policy or to the governing body any changes it considers appropriate;
- advise the governing body of the impact on the curriculum of any or proposed changes in staffing, finance, pastoral, facilities and administrative arrangements in the school;
- consider how the curriculum could be enhanced for the benefit of children/students and the broader community, in particular by engaging parents and the community more actively in the education partnership;
- review and update the governors' risk register;
- undertake such other responsibilities and work as the governing body may from time to time ask of it.

Reporting arrangements should be established between all sub-committees/task and finish groups, and the full governing body in order to ensure accountability for any actions and decisions taken within the small groups on behalf of the governing body as a whole. If there are several sub-committees, then consideration should also be given to how the committees should communicate with each other. The latter is to avoid duplication and any clashes between the areas covered by each committee.

CASE STUDY

A co-opted governor is a member of a sub-committee focusing on curriculum and standards in a secondary school. At the last meeting, there was a report on the latest GCSE and A level results, which when taken as a whole were very successful. However, a couple of subjects have dropped in comparison with previous years and you would like to know more about this trend. The co-opted member is keen to congratulate the school staff and students and move on to other items on the agenda.

- Consider how you might ensure that you have the opportunity to ask your questions in this committee meeting. Which of the following would be the most appropriate strategy?
  a. Ignore the issue and allow the meeting to move on.
  b. Politely ask the chair of the committee if you can ask a question about the issue you have spotted.
  c. Tackle the headteacher after the meeting to raise your questions.
  d. Raise the questions under 'any other business'.
  e. Tell the co-opted governor to stop by interrupting their praise of the results.

Feedback

All governors have a responsibility to both support and challenge (see Chapter 1 for more detailed discussion) and as a governor you need to consider when it is appropriate to do these within your role. The co-opted governor is right to praise good results as they take hard work by students and staff to achieve. However, when you have spotted a change in trends, it is your responsibility to ask about why these changes have taken place. So (a) is not an option if you are to fulfil your responsibilities. Opting for (c) or (d) might appear to be discharging your responsibilities, yet (c) means this is not formally recorded in any way, nor is the response heard or read by the whole governing body. Point (e) would put a governor in the position of breaching the code of conduct and being impolite.

The most appropriate option here is (b). The school staff may need to do some further investigation into the issue raised and so the full answer may be an action for the next meeting. However, most staff will have spotted issues with the results patterns and will have an explanation for the changes.

> **THINGS TO CONSIDER**
>
> From this look at the case study on sub-committee meetings, you will need to consider the following points.
>
> - Are you part of a sub-committee or task-and-finish group that allows you to be fully engaged and effective as a governor?
> - Are you clear about your role in any sub-committee or task-and-finish group?

> **WAYS OF WORKING**
>
> In order to be an active governor in meetings, you will need to set aside time to read all the papers ahead of time. You may find it easier to work with hard copies or you may prefer to access materials electronically. In either format, it is worth annotating the agendas and other papers. Comments in meetings can be supportive as well as challenging the assumptions made that inform decisions. Asking about the impact of any interventions or changes in practice can be a good starting point as this will ensure that staff reflect on their decision-making processes. Inspectors will be looking for this questioning during any inspection process as governance is part of the leadership and management category against which they make judgements. (See Chapter 8 for further details.)

Chapter 6
GOVERNORS' ROLE IN MONITORING

Introduction

This chapter provides further detail about different ways of monitoring and should be read in conjunction with Chapter 4, where specific roles are discussed. This chapter looks at visits to schools, exploring data, looking at books and talking to children/students. It offers some examples of templates that can be adapted to meet your needs but will guide your visits and questions. Governors must know their schools in order to maintain robust accountability and to be able to monitor and call the school leadership to account. There are a number of ways to fulfil this obligation, some (although not all) of which should be carried out during the school day to see the school in action.

> **KEY IDEAS FOR EXPLORATION**
>
> - Monitoring requires preparation for the agreed focus with schools and is ideally linked to the school's development plan (SDP) or improvement plan (SIP).
> - Templates can be used to guide your monitoring exploration.
> - Findings can be reported to school staff and other governors. What is the best way to do this?

Tours of the school

A tour of the school with staff and children/students can give you a picture of the site and is a good starting point for a new governor/trustee. Although this tour can be completed outside teaching time, being around as classrooms and other facilities are in use helps to see issues that may be discussed at meetings and allows you to collect information. It can also generate questions about operational matters to help you understand and, where appropriate, challenge the school's leadership. If you are a safeguarding governor, a tour of the site will allow you to see how visitors are greeted, checked in and briefed about safeguarding. It will also enable you to check the site for a vulnerable access point such as fences. Staff and children/students giving tours can emphasise different aspects of school life and provide different perspectives on issues such as changing classes in a secondary school or the changing facilities in either primary or secondary schools. Such visits are often used partly to monitor the premises and conduct a health and safety check. After these visits, a report is required to indicate follow-up actions to put things right where necessary.

Visits to schools

Visits to schools during the working day give any governor/trustee a good picture of what is going on and increase their knowledge of the school and its context. This means that when items are discussed at meetings, they know about facilities and working practices. As a governor, you are not visiting to inspect; instead, this is part of the process to monitor the school's effectiveness and to act as critical friend to members of the teaching and associated staff. You should never turn up to a school to visit unannounced – preparation is required.

Preparation for the visit

Visits should be a productive use of everyone's time, so they need to be targeted towards specific aspects of school life. It should be agreed with the headteacher what the focus should be and this should link to the SDP/SIP.

Ahead of the visit as a governor, you will need to:

- read the aspect on the SDP/SIP that is linked to the visit and identify what the school is aiming to improve;
- make sure you have your badge available to wear on your visit;
- have an agreed format for recording your observations and conversations;
- have something to write on and with so you can make brief notes during the visit;
- ensure that if you are going to talk to children/students, this has been agreed in advance;
- check that you know about the safeguarding procedures and who to contact if necessary;
- agree a date and time for the visit and ensure you are available, arriving at the school before the scheduled time so you are ready to begin when required;
- ideally agree to visit with other governors so you can discuss what you have seen afterwards.

Below are examples of schedules related to specific areas of SDP/SIP for primary schools. Table 6.1 was designed to look specifically at Key Stage (KS) 2 reading, which had been a focus for the school's development and this visit was to review the evidence that could be seen of the changes. Table 6.2 was developed to focus on the classroom environment to see whether this was supporting reading in KS2. Table 6.3 was intended to guide conversations with teaching assistants (TAs), again specifically around their work supporting children with their reading. Table 6.4 was agreed upon as the focus for looking at mathematics across the whole school. Table 6.5 focused on looking at the classroom environment to see whether this was supporting mathematics learning and teaching across the school. Table 6.6 shows a more general visit pro forma that could be used in any educational phase.

Table 6.1 Reading in KS 2 – alongside these questions you could ask the child to read a couple of pages to you

Questions	Year					
	1	2	3	4	5	6
Did you choose this book or was this chosen for you? What kind of books do you like to read?						
Do you have you a favourite story?						
Have you ever read a series about the same characters?						
Do you ever write reviews of the books you have read?						
When do you read during the school day?						
When you have finished reading a book and you are not sure what to read next, how do you decide what to read? Does anyone suggest books to you?						
What do you do when you come across a word about which you are unsure? What strategies do you use to help you find out how to read a new word?						
Are there any books you would like to be able to read that aren't available in the school?						

Table 6.2 Reading environment

Questions	Year					
	1	2	3	4	5	6
What is labelled in the classroom?						
Is there a working wall display for English? (This is a display that the children could use as a resource during lessons.)						
Are there fiction and/or non-fiction books on display?						
Is there anything on display to encourage reading – such as book reviews or work related to a particular book or poem?						
Are reading books on the children's tables?						

Table 6.3 Questions for teaching assistants (TAs)

Questions	Year					
	1	2	3	4	5	6
Do you support reading in the classroom? If so how?						
Who do you work with on their reading?						
What strategies do you use to help children read unfamiliar words?						
What was the last children's book you read?						

Table 6.4 Mathematics

Questions		Year						
		R	1	2	3	4	5	6
Which area of mathematics is being taught? Is there a clear mathematical focus for the lesson/activity? Is there a clear structure to the lesson that links previous lessons with the current one?								
Is there any evidence of the development of fluency? (This is the ability to recall mathematical facts and concepts quickly and accurately, and use that knowledge in other aspects of mathematics.) Four aspects of fluency are flexibility, appropriate choice of strategies, efficiency and accuracy								
Are children able to talk about the connections between what they have learnt previously and what they are doing today?								
Are all children included in the lesson/activity? How are different abilities being catered for?								
Are there activities available for children who complete the tasks quickly?								
Do you have any other comments?								

Table 6.5 Classroom environment

Questions		Year						
	R	1	2	3	4	5	6
Is there a working wall display for mathematics? (This is a display that the children could use as a resource during lessons and may be used by the teacher to reinforce key ideas.)								
Is there practical equipment to support the mathematics activities in the lesson – concrete, pictorial and abstract (CPA)?								
Are the children working in groups or independently?								
Are there opportunities for children to explore mathematical vocabulary? Answer questions in full sentences? Explore mathematical definitions?								

Table 6.6 A more general visit pro forma that could be used in any educational phase

Governor name:	
School:	
Role/area of specialism (This could be safeguarding, SEND, chair, e-safety, link with a subject area or other.)	
Date of visit:	
Staff member visited:	
Visit type: (Tour, visits to classes, conversations, meetings)	
Agreed focus of visit:	
Issues and key questions discussed:	
Comments: Any issues or concerns as a result of the visit. (Where this is the case, please discuss these with the headteacher before completing.)	
Signed: Date:	

During the visit

During a visit, you should ensure you do the following.

- Sign in and out at the reception and wear a governor's badge as identification of your role.
- When applicable, check with teachers before speaking to children/students and ask the children/students whether you can talk to them as a courtesy.

- Don't talk to children/students when the teacher is teaching the whole class as this is an important part of the instruction for any lesson.
- Remember to remain as an observer. Do not pass comment on classroom practice or any specific incidents that happen.
- Remember that you are not inspecting so you are not there to judge teaching methods, assess the quality of teaching or comment on the extent of learning.
- Use the agreed recording method during the visit.
- If you have any concerns, these should be raised with the headteacher or senior leadership team at the end of the visit.
- Always record any safeguarding concerns, no matter how small these might appear to be.
- Acknowledge the organisation required for your visit and thank the staff and children/students involved at the end.

After the visit

The following points provide guidance for what to do after your visit.

- Ask for any further clarification of things you might have observed.
- Give your own impressions of what you saw.
- Provide any positive comments you have about how children/students move around the school, talk about their lessons or respond to the staff.
- Raise any issues that seem to have developed.
- Use the agreed reporting method to share your notes with the other governors.
- Try to complete your report within a week of your visit.

Governors take in part in other activities

Formally planned visits are only one way to monitor activities in school. It is possible for governors to join in with other events. Table 6.7 gives some ideas of these and what you may be able to monitor as a result of your attendance.

Table 6.7 Additional events that governors could attend

Event	Role of governor	Monitoring opportunity
Open day/evening	Meet prospective parents and children/students. Answering questions and publicising the school.	The questions asked will give you information about how the school is seen in the community and what potential parental issues may exist.
Parents evening	Meeting parents and children/students. Answering questions and publicising the school. Administering questionnaires where appropriate.	The questions asked will give you information about how the school is seen in the community and what parental/children/student issues may exist.
Sporting events	Here you could be helping with organising activities and children/students.	This gives you an opportunity to see how the children/students are organised, how they behave and how the staff manage the event.
Trips	An additional adult who has been appropriately checked.	This gives you an opportunity to see how the children/students are organised, how they behave and how the staff manage the event.

GOVERNORS' ROLE IN MONITORING 111

> **CASE STUDY**
>
> You visit the school and find the office door open and the computer displaying information about children/students.
>
> - Consider what you would do as a result of seeing this on entry to the school. Which of the following would be the most appropriate strategy and why?
>   a. Ignore what you have seen and carry on with the visit.
>   b. Find the headteacher or senior leadership team and DSL to report a safeguarding and a General Data Protection Regulation (GDPR) breach.
>   c. Complete the appropriate colour safeguarding form or electronic system if you have access.
>   d. Close the office door.
>   e. Cover the computer screen.

Feedback

Option (a) is not an option as safeguarding is everyone's responsibility. You would therefore need to report that there are no staff in the office, resulting in a potential lack of security of the site. Concealing the information on the screen with a card and/or closing the office door would prevent anyone else from seeing the data. Check with the school's leadership about staff training and guidance to ensure this does not occur again.

Exploring data

Education is a data-rich system and governors are likely to be presented with data about the progress and achievements of children/students. One key issue with this data is that it is often presented as percentages, which at first glance would appear to make things easy to evaluate; however, in a small school with 32 children in a class, every child is worth just over 3 per cent whereas when looking at data with large cohorts, students can be worth a much smaller percentage. This can mean that if a child/student is absent when assessment takes place, it can make a significant difference to the overall percentages.

All schools have their own data sets but they also receive information about the achievements of similar schools and national data so the leadership can analyse the individual school's results against the other figures. This can be challenging as, although year-on-year improvements are good to see, each cohort of children/students is different from others in terms of their prior knowledge and experiences, gender balance and numbers with additional needs and this means there are likely to be variations.

Governors are looking at trends in data – for example, asking why a subject at secondary level has lower results than previously. There could be good reasons why results have changed, including changes in the curriculum, staffing or numbers of students taking this subject as an option at GCSE level. If there are concerns, governors would be asking what measures the school is putting into place to raise the achievement level in the subject identified.

As with much of the information in education, abbreviations are often applied to data sets and it is worth asking for a glossary of these to help you read any papers for meetings that include data.

The kinds of information presented to governors include:

- reception baseline assessment (RBA) and SATs;
- national tests such as phonics screening, multiplication tables at primary level;
- GCSE progress and attainment (results);
- A level, BTEC, T levels at secondary level;
- attendance.

These are usually broken down into gender groups, SEND, PPG and LAC in order to identify variations and gaps between groups. Governors need to be asking questions about the gaps in achievement between groups and what measures the school is putting in place to reduce the gaps in those areas.

Table 6.8 is an illustration of the kinds of data you might expect to see in a report about the use of the Pupil Premium Grant (PPG) monies and which groups of students, in this case at a secondary school, attract this funding.

Table 6.8 Example of data on the use of the Pupil Premium Grant (PPG)

	2019–20	2020–21	2021–22	2022–23
Students on roll	1260	1270	1275	1272
Pupil Premium (FSM6)	129	116	198	200
Child looked after	5	5	5	8
Child previously looked after	13	10	15 (11 funded)	15
Service child	3	5	5	2
Grant allocation	£139,430	£120,160	£180,535	£239,430

This table shows actual numbers of students rather than percentages as the total amount of money a school receives depends on the number of students in each category. Changes in the cost of living and numbers of families where the adults are not in work are likely to be factors that affect the numbers of students who are eligible for free school meals (FSM).

Table 6.9 is an example of the comparison between disadvantaged students and non-disadvantaged students in Year 11 (45 students, 15 per cent). Attainment 8 is a way of measuring how well pupils do in Key Stage 4, at age 16 across subjects taken at GCSE; EBACC is a specific set of subjects including English, mathematics, science, a foreign language and a humanities subject (either history or geography) but doesn't include all exams taken by individual students.

Table 6.9 Comparison between disadvantaged students and non-disadvantaged students in Year 11

	Disadvantaged	Non-disadvantaged	Gap
Total attainment 8	43	60	−17
Average attainment 8	4.10	6.10	−2
Total progress 8	0.29	0.85	−0.56
Progress 8 English	81	79	1.0
Progress 8 mathematics	70.4	67	3.4
Progress 8 EBACC	56	76	−20

From these data, governors could see that English and mathematics are successful in supporting disadvantaged students to do well though the overall gap in attainment and progress is lower for this group.

Questions to ask might include:

- how many of these students opt for a foreign language?
- what other subjects have the students in this group chosen as their options?

Analysing reports and presentations

As part of most governing body meetings, there will be presentations from staff in school and reports to read. Part of the monitoring process for governors is to ask questions about these during the meeting. If access is given to the materials ahead of the meeting, it is possible to formulate questions to ask during the meeting.

School development plan/school improvement plan (SDP/SIP)

The school's development or improvement plan is the key document that sets out the strategic direction of developments over the course of the academic year. As identified earlier, the plan is likely to be separated into the four aspects that Ofsted inspects.

1. Quality of education.
2. Personal development.
3. Behaviour and attitudes.
4. Leadership and management.

Under each of those there will be areas for development/improvement. In a secondary school, the areas are likely to range across the key stages and potentially have governor sub-committees identified as part of monitoring the progress.

Table 6.10 shows examples of the headings you might expect to see in an SDP/SIP as this the format is determined by the school/MAT. You are likely to see either of the last two rows on the plan but not both.

Table 6.10 Examples of headings in an SDP/SIP

Key stage	Staff responsible	Focus	Action	Milestones Christmas	Milestones Easter	Milestones Summer	Governor Sub-committee
Target	Impact			Strategies		Timescale	Evaluation
Intent	Implementation			Intended impact	Responsibility		Impact

As you can see, only the first example indicates a role for governors as a separate column. This is because this comes from a secondary school and there are sub-committees that take a lead in reviewing the content of areas linked to their terms of reference. The situation is likely to be different in a small school that is part of a MAT where the governance does not have separate sub-committees with differing responsibilities.

Prior to writing the SDP/SIP, the leadership team will have completed an annual self-evaluation form (SEF), which is a review of the previous year though the process of self-evaluation that goes on throughout the year. There are specific points in the year where assessment data are available, including comparison information. The latter comparison is referred to as benchmarking and made against local and national data, against similar schools – those that have children/students with similar characteristics – and looking at comparisons with the school's own data over time.

The SEF includes a review of assessment results and data about attendance, and follows the four aspects from Ofsted. Under quality of education, there will be a review of the curriculum, the intent, implementation and impact.

- *Intent:* this is the curriculum framework for setting out the aims of a programme of education, including the knowledge and skills to be gained at each stage.
- *Implementation:* how the curriculum is taught at subject and class level.
- *Impact:* what learners have learned, and the skills they have gained and can apply; partially judged through assessment results.

Ideally, governors should be able to contribute to the discussion about the SEF or at least ask questions about the information in the form prior to the compilation of the development plan. Governors can then ask about where (or whether) the SEF judgements have been moderated, perhaps by a school improvement partner. Some scrutiny of the SEF is essential so governors can be assured of the accuracy of the evidence and therefore the identification of appropriate areas for improvement. It may be possible for a small working party of governors to attend a meeting with the senior leadership team as they review the SEF and develop the plans.

Below are possible questions to ask about SDP/SIP, although this will depend on the document you are reading.

- How often is the SDP/SIP reviewed and by whom?
- How is the plan communicated to all staff?
- Are there cost implications of the areas identified?
- How are governors involved in the review of items on the plan?
- Is it clear what success will look like and does each item have milestones to show what progress will have been made at key points?
- Are there any implications for specific resources required to meet the targets?
- Is it clear which items may have been rolled over from the previous year and why?
- As a result of the target areas, are there implications for staff development to ensure these targets are met?
- At what point in the year is the SEF completed for the next round of plans?
- Is the plan available on the school's website?

CASE STUDY

A governor with a business background has attended a meeting about the completion of the SEF and the subsequent plan for action, and is concerned that not all areas identified as weaknesses are reflected in the plan. This governor feels that all the weaknesses should be included in the final version of the school's improvement plan.

Feedback

When you are used to working in a particular way, it can be hard to see that there might be different approaches. Clearly, if there are major concerns about a specific aspect of the school's performance, then those items should appear in the plan. However, all the target areas should also fit with the overall aims, values and strategic direction of the organisation. There can be a case for not focusing on an area that perhaps was in the last year's plan, and while progress has been made there is still work to do. The work may have been started and is just becoming embedded into practice, and as a consequence does not require the same level of attention as previously so doesn't roll over from one year to another. Another issue to consider is that areas of strength may appear in the plan to further strengthen this aspect of the school and grow a unique selling point.

> **THINGS TO CONSIDER**
>
> - How could you gain more knowledge about the process of the self-evaluation and planning cycle in the school?
> - What are the values and perspectives you bring to this process from your prior experience?
> - How could these influence your responses?
> - How do the areas identified in the school development plan fit with the overall vision for improvement?
> - Can you see clear success criteria for the target areas in the plan and where and how governors could be involved in monitoring progress?

Discussion with teachers

Having a conversation with a subject lead or head of department can give governors insights into specific subjects within the curriculum. You might arrange to talk to a member of staff as part of the role of link governor.

Table 6.11 Subject leader questions from primary phase

Question	Notes
What are the strengths and areas for development in your subject?	
Does the subject curriculum match or exceed the breadth of the National Curriculum?	
How is your subject timetabled across school?	
How do you evidence progress in your subject?	
Is challenge understood in terms of the demand of the curriculum end-points?	
Does curriculum planning identify small enough component steps so all children can achieve ambitious end-points?	
How can you assess and demonstrate progression across key stages?	
How is this monitored?	
What are children learning?	
Why do you teach what you do?	
How do you ensure there is a sequence of learning?	
How do you assess children's prior knowledge?	
How do you ensure that staff have good subject knowledge?	
How do you provide support to staff who need it?	

Table 6.11 is an example of subject leader questions from the primary phase that could be used to talk to a head of department in a secondary school with the addition of some questions about examination classes and revision.

Talking to children/students

Talking to children/students can form part of visits to look at specific subjects, but it can also be a specific task to review aspects of well-being, for example. You could also be asked to talk to a panel of children/students to gain their views about particular topics such as proposed changes in the school or their views about bullying. You will need to be aware that some children/students find it easier to talk to adults than others. Talking to a group of children/students – sometimes called a focus group – can allow the children/students to feel more comfortable about sharing their views. Explaining your role and why you feel their voices are important is a good start. Try to ask clear questions that encourage children/students to talk about their experiences as this will allow you to listen closely.

Table 6.12 presents some examples of questions focusing on any subject that could be used in any age phase.

Table 6.12 Questions focusing on any subject for any age phase

Question	Notes
What are you learning about in XXX today?	
Why are you doing this?	
How does this link with what you learnt last week?	
How does this link with other learning that you have done?	

Question	Notes
How often do you do XXX?	
What skills or knowledge have you learnt? How does your teacher help you to develop these?	
What is your favourite thing about the subject?	

WAYS OF WORKING

Monitoring can take a variety of forms, as can be seen in this chapter – which should be read in conjunction with Chapters 4 and 5 to give a full picture of the process of governance at work.

In order to be effective at monitoring as a governor, you will need to:

- consider a range of strategies for monitoring;
- ensure that this includes visiting the school when you can during school time;
- observe the relevant protocols for visits, conversations, meetings and ensure these are pre-planned;
- listen carefully in order to understand the issues from the perspectives of staff, children/students and parents;
- try to attend training associated with your specific role as this will give you an opportunity to meet and talk to governors from other schools as well as to learn from the training;
- visit the school and meet with the key staff as regularly as possible;
- provide notes and updates for the full governing body.

Chapter 7
SCHOOL GOVERNORS AND CONTROLLING BODIES

Introduction

School governors do not operate in isolation, but rather in partnership with a range of other organisations. This chapter provides more detail about each of these organisations and the interrelationship between those described here and the governors supporting individual schools.

The importance of looking outside individual schools is directly related to being aware of the 'bigger picture'. This is not necessarily organisations and/or policies over which governors may have any influence, but the impact of these are felt in individual schools. These also are essential in the development of long-term strategy, which is a core responsibility of the governance functions.

Department for Education

The Department for Education (DfE) is the central government's ministerial department that oversees education across the country. Like other government departments, this department is led by a minister in charge of the portfolio covered by the area, which often includes more aspects than just schools. The department is run under the minister's leadership by civil servants who enact the legislation and policies of the government. Currently, the Department for Education is responsible for children's services and education, including early years, schools, higher and further education policy, apprenticeships and wider skills in England. The breadth of this remit has varied over time. It is responsible for:

- teaching and learning for children in the early years and in primary schools;
- teaching and learning for young people in secondary schools;
- teaching, learning and training for young people and adults in apprenticeships, traineeships and further education;
- teaching and learning for young people and adults in higher education;
- supporting professionals who work with children, young people and adult learners;
- helping disadvantaged children and young people to achieve more;
- making sure local services protect and support children.

Further information can be found at www.gov.uk/government/organisations/department-for-education/about.

The department influences every educational establishment through its policy setting, which includes everything from changes to national examinations to staffing ratios in nursery provision. It produces a vast array of publications on all matters related to education and it can be a challenge to keep up to date with all this material. Changes in the ministerial responsibilities and/or changes in government can result in significant reviews. As a public service, there are few periods during which no changes are announced.

Local education authority

In England, each local education authority (LEA) is responsible for all the schools that are not academies. LEAs are also responsible for ensuring that there are sufficient places in schools across their area for all children/students regardless of which organisations run the individual schools. The authority has a responsibility to ensure appropriate education and care for all children in the area who have special educational needs, particularly those children and young people who have education and healthcare plans (EHCPs) or who are being recommended for granting these plans to support their education. In addition, they are responsible for arranging suitable education for permanently excluded pupils, and for other pupils who – because of illness or other reasons – would not receive suitable education without such arrangements being made. This is known as alternative provision (AP). Local education authorities are reviewed by a joint inspection by Ofsted and the Care Quality Commission (CQC) of the local area to judge its effectiveness in implementing the SEND reforms set out in the *Children and Families Act 2014* (UK Government, 2014). As part of this joint inspection process, the inspection team visits a range of different types of schools in the area to make their judgements about the provision for SEND across the local area. This inspection process cuts across the range of organisations working with individual schools. As a result of the legal responsibilities still placed on local authorities, even when schools become academies and/or part of MATs, there is still a relationship that must be maintained.

Academy

An academy is a state-run school but it is independent of the local authority. Academies are funded by the government. Schools in this category have more autonomy over the curriculum, school terms, the school day and teachers' pay. Individual academies are still subject to Ofsted inspections and ratings in exactly the same way as council-run schools. Academies are seen to be subject to greater accountability than council-run schools because of increased financial regulation. Some schools have chosen to become academies but if a school funded by the local authority is judged as 'inadequate' by Ofsted, then it must become an academy regardless of the school's or parents' wishes. Becoming an academy is the first necessary step to joining a MAT.

If you are a chair of governors and you have started the conversation to convert to an academy, there is a set procedure that includes:

- registering your interest with the DfE;
- becoming familiar with the financial handbook, currently available at www.gov.uk/guidance/academy-trust-handbook;
- reading the good practice guide for academy trusts, currently available at www.gov.uk/government/publications/multi-academy-trusts-establishing-and-developing-your-trust; this is so any academy meets the criteria to be approved by regional directors;
- meeting with parents, staff and all other stakeholders to explore concerns;
- hold a governing body meeting to pass a resolution to convert (with a record of the vote);
- prepare the application;
- conduct a statutory consultation with all parents and staff;
- inform the local authority;
- appoint a solicitor to act for the new organisation;
- open a bank account in the new academy name;
- complete and return a land questionnaire (this is to check any shared use of ground and facilities);
- complete and submit your draft memorandum and articles of association;
- complete and submit your draft funding arrangements;
- set up the trust;
- register at Companies House;
- appoint academy trustees;
- decide whether the academy will have its own local governing body or whether arrangements for governance will change – particularly if the school is becoming part of a MAT.

> **CASE STUDY**
>
> The governors of a school are keen to move away from the local authority and have been undertaking informal discussions with a locally run MAT, which is interested in the school joining the trust. Members of the governors and staff want to make changes to the school curriculum.

Feedback

It is important that all interested parties are not only made aware of the discussions prior to any application for conversion but that they have opportunities to ask questions and that the governors are able to address concerns. This can be a particular issue for staff who still have contracts with the local authority and may have questions about pensions and the terms and conditions of their employment. From a governance perspective, there may be changes to the governance structures, so it is worth governors exploring the potential losses and gains that conversion may bring.

Some of the best advice for governors and school leaders as a starting point for discussions about conversion to academy status comes from the Department for Education.

> *When making any decision about the future direction of the school, governors should always evaluate:*
>
> - *what is in the best interests of the children and young people and the wider community;*
> - *what is in the best interests of the staff and leadership team of the schools to develop and sustain great teaching and leadership;*
> - *what the school can bring to the academy trust and share with other schools, which would help them all to develop further;*

- *what the school can gain from an academy trust, including what it needs in order to be able to sustain and improve educational outcomes and financial sustainability.*

(Department for Education, 2021, p 10)

> **THINGS TO CONSIDER**
>
> - What benefits will conversion bring to the school as a whole?
> - How can the school retain its position in the local community if it becomes part of a much larger organisation (MAT)?
> - What might be the disadvantages for local governance?
> - How might relationships between governors and the school change with a conversion?
> - How might relationships change with parents?

Multi-academy trust

Multi-academy trusts (MATs) are charities that have the responsibility for running a number of academies, which are funded by the government. They cannot, as charities, be run for financial profit and any surplus must be reinvested in the trust. Advantages can include the schools working in partnership with each other where appropriate, sharing staff, curriculum expertise and effective teaching practices to deliver the best outcomes for children/students. While other types of school partnerships can be effective and there are many examples of this for local authority schools, the key difference with academy trusts is that there is shared accountability for standards across the trust; all schools within the trust support each other and the trust is accountable for them all. In many ways, the trust takes on the role that the local authority had regarding the schools under its remit. The Department for Education's National and Regional Schools Commissioners and their teams, together with the Education and Skills Funding Agency, provides robust educational and financial oversight of all academy trusts. Individual schools are still inspected by Ofsted to ensure an appropriate education for all children/students in each school.

Free school

Free schools are funded directly by the government and are not run by the local authority. They have more control over how they operate. They do not have to follow the national curriculum. The school must cater for all abilities, so cannot use academic selection processes – for example, like a grammar school.

Free schools can:

- set their own pay and conditions for staff;
- change the length of school terms and the school day.

Free schools are run on a not-for-profit basis and can be set up by groups such as:

- charities;
- universities;
- independent schools;
- community and faith groups;
- teachers;
- parents;
- businesses.

There are two types of free schools. The first is university technical colleges (UTCs), which specialise in subjects such as engineering and construction. They teach these subjects along with business skills and using information technology (IT). These are sponsored by universities, employers and/or further education colleges. The second type is referred to as studio schools (usually with around 300 pupils), teaching mainstream qualifications through project-based learning. This means working in realistic situations as well as learning academic subjects. Students work with local employers and a personal coach, and follow a curriculum designed to give them the skills and qualifications they need in work, or to take up further education. By law, both categories of free schools are academies. The difference is that these are not existing schools as most academies are new schools.

Other organisations that influence schools

Services to schools

Assumptions are made by services such as water, energy and road maintenance that all schools are still linked to the local authority and therefore communications are managed by the local authority. This can lead to schools that have become members of a MAT missing out on key information about work that is likely to impact on them.

> **CASE STUDY**
>
> A water company had communicated to the local authority and related councils about major work that would take place over a period of six months. The impact of this work would mean closing access to entry to the school as the work involved road closures. The water company did not contact the school directly about the work to be undertaken, and had not talked to the school about any mitigations of access or issues about the water supply during the period of work.

Feedback

As a governor, it is important to ask questions about just how informed services are about which organisations run the school with which you are working, especially if there have been changes. It is perhaps surprising that individuals and organisations are not aware of where the responsibility for schools lies. It is an aspect of the changes to schools that has not been widely publicised.

THINGS TO CONSIDER

- What are the responsibilities of the governing body under any scheme of delegation in relation to communication with outside agencies?
- How might you address queries or questions from parents about work, either in the school or close to the school, that impact access to school grounds?

WAYS OF WORKING

This chapter has explored the current position of schools and governance in different contexts; however, this can be viewed as something of a moving target for governors. Academisation was first introduced in 2000 under Tony Blair's government, and was designed to see the rebranding of schools in challenging circumstances, giving them a fresh start as new schools. The numbers of schools converting has increased, although there has been opposition to some of the changes. The government's White Paper, published in March 2022, set out its ambition to see every school in England in a multi-academy trust (MAT) or in the process of joining one by 2030. Although this bill has now been scraped, the government's plan is to continue to complete as much of the academy plans as possible without new legislation and an ongoing academy review will continue. Future plans include legislation to remove barriers for faith schools to join trusts. As a governor, you will need to be aware of your current governance context and how these plans will change the nature of your role, depending upon the scheme of delegation agreed with the specific MAT. Chapter 9 provides advice about remaining up to date and information about sources of training to retain your skillset.

References

Department for Education (2021) *Building Strong Academy Trusts: Guidance for Academy Trusts and Prospective Converters*. London: UK Government. [online] Available at: https://assets.publishing. service.gov.uk/government/uploads/system/uploads/attachment_ data/file/987336/Building_strong_academy_trusts_guidance.pdf (accessed 2 January 2023).

UK Government (2014) *Children and Families Act 2014.* [online] Available at: www.legislation.gov.uk/ukpga/2014/6/contents/enacted (accessed 15 March 2023).

Chapter 8

GOVERNANCE AND INSPECTIONS

Introduction

A key aspect of the role of governors comes to the fore when schools are inspected and the starting question is asked: '*How well do you know your school?*' This chapter explores the range of inspections that you might encounter as a governor and what might be expected of you during the inspection process. There are two main inspection procedures. The first is Ofsted inspections under section 5 of the *Education Act 2005* (UK Government, 2005) and the second is related to schools with a specific religious affiliation, which are inspected separately under section 48 of the *Education Act 2005*. Both are graded inspections, as detailed later in this chapter. Both types of inspections give little notice ahead of the visits by the inspection team, so it is worth governors always being aware of who is available if the school receives the phone call announcing the visit. This occurs the day before the visit begins. Both types of inspections require input from governors, although potentially a much wider group for the main Ofsted inspections as they have a much broader focus. While these two inspections usually occur on a rolling national cycle, parental complaints – particularly in relation to safeguarding – can trigger an inspection for your school at any point.

Under section 8 of the *Education Act 2005*, Ofsted conducts ungraded inspections, which differ from graded inspections because they do not result in individual graded judgements;

instead, they focus on determining whether the school remains the same grade as it was at its previous graded inspection. Urgent inspections are also conducted under section 8 of the *Education Act 2005*, and were previously known as inspections with no fixed designation and unannounced behaviour inspections. Ofsted may also conduct inspections under section 8 of the *Education Act 2005* in order to comply with a request from the Secretary of State under section 118(2) of the *Education and Inspections Act 2006* (UK Government, 2006) or information or advice about maintained schools and academies. They may also carry out research during inspections and these often form reports on specific aspects of education. Table 8.1 provides a summary of inspections.

Table 8.1 Summary of inspections

Section under the *Education Act 2005*	Frequency	Length of inspection	Schools	Possible outcomes
Section 5	Approx every four years	1–2 days	All	Grades given: 1 – outstanding; 2 – good; 3 – requires improvement (RI); 4 – inadequate.
Section 8	Approx every four years	1–2 days	All	Ungraded – focuses on determining whether the school remains the same grade as at the school's previous graded inspection.
Section 8(2)	As required	1–2 days usually though can be longer	Any	These are triggered by concerns or complaints.
Section 48	Three to five years		Only those designated with a religious character	Grades given: 1 – outstanding; 2 – good; 3 – requires improvement (RI); 4 – inadequate.

Ofsted inspections

The main Ofsted inspections focus on the following:

- quality of education;
- behaviour and attitudes;
- personal development;
- leadership and management;
- early years provision in schools (where appropriate);
- sixth form provision in schools (where appropriate).

When these are graded inspections, there is a grade given for each of these for the provision and an overall effectiveness grade. The grades are: 1 – outstanding; 2 – good; 3 – requires improvement (RI); and 4 – inadequate. If a school is judged as RI at its last inspection, it is a school that is not yet good but overall provides an acceptable standard of education. The school will receive a graded inspection again within a period of 30 months. If a school has been judged as RI at two successive inspections, it will be subject to monitoring from inspectors to check its progress. Ofsted will also carry out a graded inspection again within a period of 30 months of the publication of the previous graded inspection report. If a school is graded as 4 – inadequate, the school is placed in a category of concern because it either has serious weaknesses or it requires special measures. The Secretary of State for Education will issue an academy order to a maintained school judged inadequate and placed in a category of concern. The school will then become a sponsored academy. Ofsted will not usually monitor the school unless there are safeguarding concerns or there is a delay in the school becoming a sponsored academy. Academies placed in this category can be moved between MATs and then Ofsted will monitor the school's progress as with other schools.

Governors and inspection

Governance is part of the leadership and management section of the inspection. From the grade descriptors for 'good', it is possible to see how governance fits into this section – although more generally where the descriptors mention leaders, this includes governors and trustees as well as teachers.

> *Those responsible for governance understand their role and carry this out effectively. Governors/trustees ensure that the school has a clear vision and strategy, that resources are managed well and that leaders are held to account for the quality of education.*
>
> *Those with responsibility for governance ensure that the school fulfils its statutory duties, for example under the Equality Act 2010, and other duties, for example in relation to the 'Prevent' duty and safeguarding.*
>
> (Ofsted, 2022, para 417)

In an inspection, inspectors will hold the trust responsible for governance if your school is part of a MAT; if not, this will rest with the governing body of the school.

However, they are likely to ask to meet with the chair of governors and others if required. The school and governors can not only ask for further discussions but can direct inspectors to see things and hear about activities that they might not have already engaged with during their time in the school. It is important to remember that safeguarding, SEND and reading have a high profile.

Remember the core purposes of school governance (see Chapter 1 to recap on governance):

- ensuring the clarity of vision, ethos, and strategic direction;
- holding leaders to account;
- financial performance (in some MATs they will have responsibility for this) though there are specific grants for PPG and PE/sports that governors need to monitor.

Table 8.2 presents a list of potential questions that could be asked around the key areas covered by section 5 inspections. It is not an exhaustive list; rather, it is designed to help you start thinking about how you will address your role in the inspection process. The second column provides some guidance about what information is required and where this can be found.

It is difficult to provide an exact list of all the things an inspection team will be looking for, as any inspection will be tailored to the school's context and the lead inspectors first read all the school's documentation. However, the question areas in the table will suggest the areas that are most likely to come up in any conversations with the inspectors. The questions may be worded differently, but still be related to the same area, so preparing the topic rather than specific answers is the most helpful approach. It is good to give examples of things you have seen, read or taken part in to illustrate your answers.

Governors will receive a letter from the lead/sole inspector via the chair indicating the dates for the inspection and asking to meet with the chair and as many governors as possible during the inspection. Meetings with governors take place without the presence of the headteacher or staff, with the exception of the feedback meeting when all are present together. Governors are also invited to the feedback meeting at the end of the inspection process. Importantly, the outcome of the inspection is confidential at this stage and cannot be shared until the final report has been published. During the course of the inspection, a timetable will be drawn up identifying times when the lead/sole inspector or team wishes to meet specific governors and trust members. All parent governors will also receive a survey to complete about the school. If governors are not able to meet the inspectors face to face, they are invited to contact the lead/sole inspector directly, either in person or by telephone, if there is anything about the school or the work of governors that they would like to discuss during the inspection. This acknowledges that governors are volunteers and have other commitments, which may make attendance at short notice more difficult.

Table 8.2 Sample inspection questions

Questions	Comments
General information How well do you know your school?	Inspectors will expect you to be able to talk about your school in general terms and have more specific knowledge if you have responsibility for a key area such as safeguarding or SEND.
School values	You should know the vision statement of the school and the aims set out in all the school's documentation and website.
Numbers on roll	This does not need to be the exact number, as children/students do move in year; however, knowing roughly how many children/students are enrolled is helpful.
Percentage disadvantaged, SEND, EHCP	Again the exact number is less important than how these numbers relate to national figures and whether or not they are a true reflection of the needs of children/students.
Pupil admission	This is the Pupil Admission Number (PAN), which is related to the capacity of the school.
Year groups	It is important from governors to know the age and year group covered by the school.

Number of children who have left school for home schooling or other provision	Although there are always fluctuations in the school population, with families moving in and out of the catchment area, there are concerns about the children who are missing from education (CME). This has become a much bigger issue since COVID-19, with increases in the number of children/students who have not returned to school. All schools should have a clear procedure in place if parents wish to withdraw their children/students from education. As a governor, you need to know that a procedure is in place and that it is used when parents take their children out of school. Again, exact numbers are not expected but you should be looking at trends in the data.
Data	You should be able to talk about the presentation of data during governors' meetings and inspectors should be able to see the questions that governors have posed – both challenging and supporting – from the minutes of meetings.
Your school's curriculum and performance data	You should be able to talk about the trends in children's/students' progress and attainment over time. It is useful to know how your school's data compare with national averages. You do not need to be able to list facts and figures for specific subjects. An analysis of these data should be reflected in the school development or improvement plan so you can talk about what the school is doing about the trends it has identified. An example post COVID-19 has been the delay in communication and language skills of children entering school. Many children have not

Table 8.2 (continued)

Questions	Comments
	had rich language environments so schools have targeted support and activities to increase vocabulary. In secondary schools, knowledge of the successful subjects at GSCE and A level can be helpful and again provide examples of analysis and development plans.
Your school's behaviour data, including: • attendance; • sanctions, suspensions and exclusions; • searches and confiscations.	Good preparation is to re-read the behaviour policy. You should know what the trends in attendance are for your school and whether there are specific groups with lower attendance, and what is being put in place to change these behaviours. How do suspensions and exclusion figures compare with national figures? Are there more children/students in these categories? How do these figures compare with other groups of learners, such as PPG or SEND?
Development	This is where knowledge of the content of the SDP/SIP is key to being able to answer questions in this category.
What are the strengths of the school? How do you know?	If you have taken part in discussions of the self-evaluation and development of the current plans, you will know where the school's strengths lie.
What are the areas of development? How do you know?	Areas for development are not always those where there is a negative outcome; it may be that the school is also continuing to work on areas of strength.

How do you hold leaders to account?	You can point to minutes of governors' meetings, sub-committees, and monitoring visits.
Curriculum	Clearly this is the main focus of teachers' work and governors are not expected to be experts in curriculum design. This section is more about the information you have been given and what questions you have asked, and continue to ask, about curriculum as this is not a static area.
What is the school's curriculum intent? What role did you have any shaping this intent?	The overview of curriculum intent, which is everything that needs to be considered before teaching takes place, should be on the school's website. The degree to which you may have been involved in shaping the intent will vary, and this is partly related to how long you have been a governor and when the work on the curriculum intent took place. At secondary level, you may have been involved through a curriculum sub-committee. There should be evidence in minutes of meetings through presentations and discussions.
How well is the curriculum intent embedded?	As curriculum is not static, governors should expect an update on how well the curriculum intent is embedded at least on an annual basis and there should be evidence of this in meeting minutes.
Is the curriculum narrowed in any way?	This can be focused on the breadth of the curriculum in the primary phase associated with the time allocated to specific subjects. In the secondary phase, this is often related to when students begin GCSE studies and choose options, as there are variations nationally.

Table 8.2 (continued)

Questions	Comments
Have you ensured that school leaders have created a curriculum that is appropriately ambitious and sequenced?	Sequencing is not just within subjects but also between subjects where possible to help consolidate knowledge and skills.
Are there memorable experiences for the children? Additionality?	Education does not just occur in the classroom; it includes trips, visitors to the school, experiencing new sports, music and many other activities. For governors, it is important to know what is planned and how all children/students are able to access these activities.
Safeguarding	Although there will be a governor who takes on specific responsibility for this area, this is everyone's task. Everyone should know about the policy and practices in your school.
How do you know safeguarding is effective at the school?	Evidence will include training logs, KCSIE, SCR and safe recruitment as well as induction of new children/students and staff. Questions in this area may be addressed most effectively by the governor with oversight of safeguarding, as there will be notes from governors' meetings with the designated safeguarding lead (DSL).

How do you know that statutory duties, under the *Equality Act 2010* (UK Government, 2010), such as the Prevent Duty are fulfilled at the school?	You should be able to talk about the training you have undertaken and also about reports if any referrals have been made under 'Prevent'.
Personal development How does the school support the personal development of all its students?	Across all schools, there will be a Personal Social Health Education (PSHE) curriculum associated with the sex and relationships curriculum and areas such as internet safety. In the primary phase, this is also linked to attitudes, behaviour and developing friendships. In the secondary phase, this will also include career planning, working with charities, Duke of Edinburgh Awards and public speaking, for example.
Finance How much targeted funding has your school received (eg Pupil Premium and PE and Sport Premium, PPG for all schools, PE/sports for primary only)? How is the money spent? What is the impact of the funding?	You would expect to have received reports about specific targeted grants throughout the year, demonstrating where the monies have been spent and their impact. Pupil Premium Grant (PPG) usually has a designated governor, who takes a specific interest in this grant and how it is used. This is also published on the school's website.

Table 8.2 (continued)

Questions	Comments
How is the financial security of your school monitored?	For schools within MATs, this will be addressed by the finance administrator and the trustee who has oversight of this area. For other schools, information is likely to come through reports to governing bodies.
Staff well-being and workload How do you ensure staff well-being, including that of senior leaders, is supported by the governors?	Over recent years, there have been concerns about the recruitment and retention of staff. Inspectors would be looking to see whether governors raise questions about increases in staff workload with regard to changes to planning, assessment and other areas.

If you are meeting inspectors as a group of governors, it can be useful to ask relevant governors such as the safeguarding governor to address questions on this topic and other governors to answer other questions. In a group, you are more likely to have your memory jogged by listening to others' answers and then be able to offer additional information.

CASE STUDY

A team of Ofsted inspectors has arranged to meet a group of governors as part of the inspection process. The inspector asks a question about the number of children/students who have left the school and not transferred to another school in the last year. The governors know it is not a substantial number, but no one can remember an exact figure. What should the governors do in their interview?

Feedback

As stated earlier, it is not expected that governors will know exact numbers as it is the practices and procedures that are important, as well as the identification of trends. If the governors have noticed a substantial increase in the number of children/students leaving education, then inspectors would want to see how the governors have scrutinised this information. There would be evidence in meeting minutes that would show the questions asked and the responses, follow-up actions in school and the impact of those reported. Governors should also be aware of the process undertaken by the school if children/students are missing from school. This is obviously linked to attendance and potential safeguarding concerns. There should be a protocol to demonstrate how rigorously the school checks before a pupil leaves the school. Inspectors are expecting to talk to governors who know their school, what is going on, why and how you know, and monitoring is a key part of this process. (See Chapter 6 for ways of achieving this.) As a governor, you need to familiarise yourself with all the appropriate documentation, including SEF, action plans and inspection handbooks. It is also helpful to review the possible questions you may be asked as a governor and to consider answers relating to key areas rather than rehearsing set responses.

> **THINGS TO CONSIDER**
>
> - Have you reviewed the SDP/SIP? What are the strengths and areas you have identified for development so you can talk about these with an inspector?
> - If you have a specific responsibility on the governing body/committee, what questions do you think would apply to your role?
> - Is there a plan for the governors' meetings with the inspectors? What does this plan look like?

Section 48 inspections

If the school where you are a governor is designated as having a religious character, then the denominational education and collective worship will be inspected under section 48 of the *Education Act 2005* (UK Government, 2005). These inspections are conducted in addition to Ofsted inspections. They are explained in more detail in paragraphs 58 to 63 of Ofsted's (2022) *School Inspection Handbook*. This applies to any school with a religious character. The *Schools Bill* (Department for Education, 2022) is seen to strengthen the protection for schools with specific religious character and encourage an increase in the total number of schools in this category. All schools would expect to produce a self-evaluation document, which will detail the school's work towards the expected areas of the specific faith. In addition, there is usually a requirement to offer a brief summary document or pre-inspection form for the inspectors. There are slight variations in the procedures across the differing faiths. Inspectors would expect to meet with foundation governors in particular to ask about progress towards the religious vision of the school. Although the level of detail available about each religion's inspection procedures varies, they all focus on the same key areas with the same rigour.

Muslim schools

For Muslim schools, the Association of Muslim Schools (AMS) UK is the body accredited by the Department for Education to undertake inspections for religious education in Muslim schools in the United Kingdom. Further details of the AMS can be found at https://ams-uk.org/section-48-inspections.

The inspection process focuses on the following areas in each school:

- the overall effectiveness and efficiency of the provision of religious education (RE) in the school;
- the quality of leadership, management and governance of RE in the school;
- the achievement and progress over time of pupils in their RE at the school;
- the quality of teaching and learning in delivering the RE curriculum of the school, including standards of behaviour and the quality of assessment of pupils' progress;
- the quality of the Islamic curriculum itself, including meeting the statutory requirement for a daily act of collective worship;
- the quality of provision for spiritual, moral, social and cultural development of pupils, including the impact on the whole school community.

Christian schools

Christian schools fall into the following categories:

- Roman Catholic;
- Church of England;
- Methodist;
- Greek Orthodox.

Catholic schools

For Catholic schools from November 2019, the Bishops' Conference unanimously agreed to a National Framework for the Inspection of Catholic schools, colleges and academies. Full details are available about the training of inspectors and the procedures and judgements at https://catholicschoolsinspectorate.org.uk/about-us.

The inspection covers three key areas with sub-sections, as seen in Table 8.3.

Church of England and Methodist schools

The Statutory Inspection of Anglican and Methodist Schools (SIAMS) is the Church of England and Methodist Church's approach to the section 48 inspection. These inspections focus on the impact of the church school's Christian vision. This involves looking at the school's Christian vision, the provision the school makes to achieve this vision and its effectiveness in enabling all pupils to flourish. Church schools may do this in a variety of ways, so the inspectors are not looking for a specific approach but rather that there is evidence of the distinctiveness and effectiveness of the Christian character and ethos. Inspectors will look at the context and how the school works within this to achieve its aims. The evaluation schedule has one inspection question: *'How effective is the school's distinctive Christian vision, established and promoted by leadership at all levels, in enabling pupils and adults to flourish?'*

Table 8.3 The key judgement summaries for Catholic schools

Catholic life and mission		Identity, charism and mission. Sense of worth. Moral development. Catholic social teaching. Respect for self and others. Chaplaincy.
		Identity, charism and mission staff commitment. Sense of community and inclusivity. Staff as role models. Pastoral care. Physical environment. Chaplaincy (pupils and staff).
		Catholic life and mission in school policy. Engagement with diocese, including parish partnership with parents. Commitment to Catholic social teaching. Respect for the rights and dignities of employees. Catholic curriculum. Governors' ambition. Self and pupil evaluation. Continuing professional development (CPD) and induction of new staff.
Religious education		Development of knowledge, understanding and skills. Progress (including of groups). Religious literacy. Knowledge recall and questions. Independence and concentration. Quality of pupil work. Engagement and enjoyment. Self-assessment. Attainment.
		Subject and pedagogical knowledge. Expectations. Planning effective questioning. Celebration and feedback. Spiritual and moral development. Variety and resources.
		RECD. Core parity. CPD subject leader curriculum Design. Pupils' needs. Enrichment. Self-evaluation.
Collective worship		Pupil engagement. Pupil participation. Collaborative planning. Pupil evaluation. Influence on school life and curriculum. Impact.
		Centrality. Daily pattern and rhythm. Variety. Use of scripture. Staff skill and role-modelling. Creativity. Use of space. Involvement of families and parish(es).
		Impact of policy. Strategy for development of skills and participation. Sacraments. Holy days and other significant days. CPD and formation leaders' knowledge and skill. Impact of leadership. Resourcing self-evaluation.

This is explored through seven strands:

1. vision and leadership;
2. wisdom, knowledge and skills;
3. character development: hope, aspiration and courageous advocacy;
4. community and living well together;
5. dignity and respect;
6. the impact of collective worship;
7. the effectiveness of religious education.

One overall grade is awarded, reflecting the contribution of these strands to the flourishing of pupils and adults in a church school. In addition, a standalone grade is awarded in all schools for collective worship and in voluntary aided (VA) schools and former VA schools for religious education (RE). This grade is based on teaching and learning alone.

From September 2023, the approach taken by SIAMS inspectors shifted from focusing on lists of inspection criteria to exploring with school leaders in depth whether and how, through its theologically rooted Christian vision, the school is living up to its foundation as a church school, enabling children/students and adults to flourish. There are six inspection questions (IQs) for voluntary controlled and former voluntary controlled schools, and seven for voluntary aided and former voluntary aided schools. The seventh addresses teaching and learning in religious education.

The 2023 inspection questions are:

  IQ1 How does the school's theologically rooted Christian vision enable pupils and adults to flourish?
  IQ2 How does the curriculum reflect the school's theologically rooted Christian vision?

IQ3 How is collective worship enabling pupils and adults to flourish spiritually?

IQ4 How does the theologically rooted Christian vision create a culture in which pupils and adults are treated well?

IQ5 How does the theologically rooted Christian vision create an active culture of justice and responsibility?

IQ6 Is the religious education curriculum effective (with reference to the expectations set out in the Church of England's Statement of Entitlement for Religious Education)?

IQ7 What is the quality of religious education in VA and former VA schools, or in former voluntary controlled schools in which denominational religious education is taught?

Further information on SIAMS can be found on the Church of England website at www.churchofengland.org/about/education-and-schools/church-schools-and-academies/siams-inspections.

Greek Orthodox schools

The majority of Greek schools are part time and sit outside full-time education. However, the small number of Greek full-time schools are inspected under section 48 by the relevant Catholic diocese.

Seventh Day Adventist schools

The Education Department of the British Union Conference of the Seventh Day Adventist takes responsibility for conducting the section 48 inspections for the small number of schools with this specific religious vision, even though all the schools listed are independent schools. Further details can be found at https://adventist.uk.

Jewish schools

For Jewish schools, the Department for Education has approved the Jewish Studies Education Inspection Service to train inspectors who are part of the Pikuach, the Board of Deputies, and this is the body responsible for inspecting Jewish education in maintained Jewish schools.

Pikuach has identified the elements that are seen in a spiritual adult, and these form the basis of their initial work for the inspection process:

- acknowledging the divine;
- awareness of spirituality in all humankind;
- experiencing spiritual awe and wonder at the world around them;
- experiencing holiness in everyday life.

Pikuach has the following three key judgement areas for its inspections:

1. quality of Jewish education;
2. Jewish personal and spiritual development;
3. leadership and management.

Inspections will look for evidence to make judgements against these three areas in the report. Further information can be found at www.pikuachuk.org.

Sikh schools

Sikh schools are inspected by the Network of Sikh Organisations, which trains and conducts the section 48 inspections. Further information about the network can be found at https://nsouk.co.uk.

Hindu schools

Schools with a Hindu faith character are inspected by the Krishna Avanti Trust. Further information about the Trust can be found at https://avanti.org.uk.

> **CASE STUDY**
>
> A new foundation governor gets a call that a section 48 inspection is going to take place and they are asked to meet the inspection team. The governor is not sure what to do as they have never taken part in a school inspection of any kind. What steps should they take?

Feedback

Most schools are aware of the cycle of inspections and do discuss what happens in governor meetings and/or sub-committees. As part of your induction as a new governor, you should have received information about your role and the expectations. The school should have a development plan associated with the specific religion of the school and you could take a copy of this with you to discuss in your interview with the inspectors. Hopefully, you are not alone as a foundation governor and you are able to meet the inspectors as a group, which can be supportive.

> **THINGS TO CONSIDER**
>
> - How does your school teach religious education and how does it engage in collective worship?
> - Have you visited the school, had conversations with key staff and scrutinised school policies?
> - Is the religious character of the school a regular item on the governors' meetings agendas?

→

- Have you familiarised yourself with all the appropriate documentation SEF, action plans and inspection handbooks?
- Have you reviewed the possible questions you may be asked as a governor and considered answers related to key areas?

WAYS OF WORKING

A key message from this chapter is that taking on the role as a governor/trustee means that you need to spend time getting to know the school or schools with which you are involved to be able to effectively take part in an inspection process. Inspections are a rigorous review of the school and therefore need to be taken seriously as part of governance.

References

Department for Education (2022) *Statutory Faith Protections for Academies with a Religious Character: Schools Bill Factsheet*. London: UK Government. [online] Available at: https://assets.publishing.service.gov.uk/government/uploads/system/uploads/attachment_data/file/1077815/Faith_protections_-_Schools_Bill_Factsheet.pdf (accessed 18 March 2023).

Ofsted (2022) *School Inspection Handbook*. [online] Available at: www.gov.uk/government/publications/school-inspection-handbook-eif/school-inspection-handbook#grade-descriptors-for-leadership-and-management (accessed 13 January 2023).

UK Government (2005) *Education Act 2005*. [online] Available at: www.legislation.gov.uk/ukpga/2005/18/contents (accessed 16 March 2023).

UK Government (2006) *Education and Inspections Act 2006*. [online] Available at: www.legislation.gov.uk/ukpga/2006/40/contents (accessed 16 March 2023).

UK Government (2010) *Equality Act 2010*. [online] Available at: www.legislation.gov.uk/ukpga/2010/15/contents (accessed 21 November 2022).

Chapter 9
FURTHER SUPPORT

The role of governor can be challenging in education given that, as with most public services, there are almost constant changes. This section gives you an overview of the places and organisations that are sources of support and training. All governing bodies or governance committees will keep a training log as good practice and there is usually an expectation that governors will update their safeguarding training annually, which is statutory under KCISE, as well attend at least one further training session. These expectations are identified in the code of conduct that governors sign annually. The listings in this chapter are not exhaustive, but will give you a starting point for further development of your knowledge, skills and areas of interest. Some sources require subscriptions, which is either an individual governing body decision or a trust-wide subscription that would give you a username and login to access all information. Individual subscriptions are possible with some organisations, but this means self-funding whereas school or MAT subscriptions are paid for by the organisation.

Department for Education information

All government information is freely available and you can sign up to receive updates to your governor email.

Governance guidance
www.gov.uk/guidance/guide-for-newly-opened-academies-academy-trusts-and-free-schools/governance

Understanding your data
www.gov.uk/government/publications/understanding-your-data-a-guide-for-school-governors-and-academy-trustees

Governance update
www.gov.uk/government/publications/school-governance-update

Charities and charity trustees: school governors
www.gov.uk/government/publications/charities-and-charity-trustees-school-governors

Governance handbook
www.gov.uk/government/publications/governance-handbook

Statutory policies for schools and academy trusts
www.gov.uk/government/publications/statutory-policies-for-schools-and-academy-trusts/statutory-policies-for-schools-and-academy-trusts#who-this-guidance-is-for

A Competency Framework for Governance: the knowledge, skills and behaviours needed for effective governance in maintained schools, academies, and multi-academy trusts
www.gov.uk/government/publications/governance-handbook

Local authority support and training

Governors can access support and training from the local authority, either through free services or more often through subscriptions. Some trusts subscribe to local authority training, and this is one area to ask about regardless of the type of school where you are a governor. Local authorities produce training brochures of the training for the year. They also provide updates via email to heads and chairs of governors, which is often free to subscribe to and can be helpful in finding out about what is going on in the local area. The local authority usually provides a phone support contact for governors who require advice and support with their role. Local authorities can support schools with a review of governance, and this is often detailed in the training brochure.

> **CASE STUDY**
>
> A governor from a MAT school was invited to a local authority briefing about SEND, which they weren't sure would be appropriate or useful. However, this was a free virtual briefing so they decided to attend.

Feedback

The briefing detailed information about the LA charter for SEND as a result of the last LA Ofsted/CQC inspection of SEND provision in the area. The governor came away from the meeting with information about training, and sources of SEND support for schools, parents and governors. It also enabled them to ask questions about SEND on their next visit to school and to ensure that the charter for displayed prominently in the school entrance and on class platforms. Training and/or briefing sessions always add to your knowledge base as a governor. This could help you if you are considering volunteering for a specific role. (See Chapter 4 for details of possible roles.)

> **THINGS TO CONSIDER**
>
> - What areas of your governor knowledge do you think could use extra training and why?
> - Do you have a governor on your board/committee who is responsible for training and have they talked to you about what is on offer? If not, talk to your chair.

MAT/trust support and training

MATs/trusts also provide email updates for heads and chairs of governors, which are linked to the schools within the trust. They also provide training – sometimes just for the individual group of schools in the MAT and sometimes more widely, although often at a cost. As all schools in MATs are academies, even though the *Governance Handbook* (Department for Education, 2020) suggests annual reviews of governance, the important aspects are to regularly audit skills of the governors, keep training logs and regularly carry out a self-evaluation of the governance. MATs usually have a role in the central services, which is either exclusively governance across the trust or a major part of their function.

Work-based governor groups

Many larger organisations such as universities, retail outlets and manufacturing groups encourage their employees to become governors as part of their community-engagement strategies. Some organisations form groups to share experiences and support individuals from the same organisation in their roles as governors. If you are currently working, it would be worth inquiring whether such a group exists in your workplace.

Other sources

While the list in Table 9.1 is not exhaustive, it does provide some ideas about where training can be found to keep you up to date.

Table 9.1 Sources for governance information.

Organisation	Web link	Comments
National Governance Association (NGA)	www.nga.org.uk	Various types of membership exist, which give limited or full access to the materials on the website. The organisation also produces books such as the *Chair's Handbook*, which can be purchased without subscription.
Governors for Schools	www.governorsforschools.org.uk	This organisation finds and places volunteers on school and academy governing boards across England and Wales. They offer some free e-learning and webinars.
Inspiring Governance	www.inspiringgovernance.org	This organisation connects skilled volunteers who are interested in serving as school governors and trustees with schools in England. It can help you find a school that is looking for governors or trustees near you.
Confederation of School Trusts	www.cstuk.org.uk	This is a national organisation and sector body for school trusts in England advocating for, connecting and supporting executive and governance leaders. A subscription is required to access all resources.

→

Table 9.1 (*continued*)

Organisation	Web link	Comments
Governors' Virtual Office	www.thegvoffice.com	This is a cloud-based tool designed specifically for school and college governing bodies. It offers a range of support and resources for a subscription fee.
Educare	www.educare.co.uk	This is a popular platform for online training. It is available through subscription.
Governor Hub	www.governorhub.com	This is popular as the platform for all governor documentation as well as a source of training and support. You can subscribe as a standalone board or as a MAT. You can join Governor Hub or add in Governor Hub Knowledge

WAYS OF WORKING

This short chapter emphasises the significant amount of support and training available for governors. Challenges arise with location and timing of training courses; however, more resources are available online and can be completed in governors' own homes when they have time available. As governing bodies/committees keep records of training undertaken, it would be useful for individual governors to check whether specific courses require refreshing as well as the last gap between attending any training. Attending face-to-face training allows for time to network with other governors, with whom sharing knowledge and experience can be as valuable as the course content. The choice of training medium can often be dictated by the amount of time you have available, but there are plenty of different options to choose from.

As an example of the impact of training, a governor with a year's experience reflected upon exactly how much had changed in what was little more than a school year. As her confidence grew in the role, she became increasingly aware of the vital importance of keeping abreast of the many changes that were on the horizon. Greater attention was paid to articles about schools and education in general in the national press and media and, through talking to other school governors, it emerged that by making time available to access some of the resources that were widely available to school governors for development, not only she but the governing body would perform better. The result was not just a growth in the understanding of the role but an increase in the ability to make appropriate contributions and the ability to ask better questions. This highlights the benefits of continuing to upskill in the role of governor.

Reference

Department for Education (2020) *Governance Handbook: Academy Trusts and Maintained Schools*. London: UK Government. [online] Available at: https://assets.publishing.service.gov.uk/government/uploads/system/uploads/attachment_data/file/925104/Governance_Handbook_FINAL.pdf (accessed 3 October 2022).

GLOSSARY OF USEFUL TERMS

This section details many of the terms you will come across either in this book or in documents associated with your role as a school governor. You can use the information in this chapter as a reference while reading this book or dip in and out of as you conduct your duties.

A levels
National examinations taken in England, Wales and Northern Ireland at the end of two years of study in schools in Year 13 (17/18 years of age). These examinations can also be taken in colleges.

Academy
A state funded school that is not under the control of the local authority.

Academy governance committee
Within some multi-academy structures, under their scheme of delegation, the governance can look quite different from that of a local authority school. Instead of a governing board, the new role of governors is indicated partially through a change in the name from governing body to committee. The governors are a committee under the overarching structure of governance across the MAT.

Academy trust
A charitable board that oversees one academy or a group of academy schools.

Action grid
Usually part of the minutes indicating actions to be taken and by whom between meetings; these are reviewed after the approval of the minutes of the previous meeting.

Agenda
The document that details the structure, items to be discussed and the timing of a governors' meeting. The usual practice is for this to be sent out to governors at least a week before the date of the meeting.

AP
Alternative provision, which is an alternative to attending school – sometimes as part of the overall provision for children/students who find full-time school difficult. It is also the provision that must be provided by the local education authority for children/students who have been permanently excluded from school. This can be face to face, home tutoring or virtual schooling.

Articles of association
This formal document sets out the management structures and how decisions are made, by whom and where in the organisation these are made in relation to an academy and its operation.

Associate member
Someone who the governors have asked to join a committee as a member, where they can have voting rights but not as part of the full governing body. They are not considered a governor.

Board of trustees
The group of individuals who deliver the three core functions of governance in a trust board.

CLA
Children looked after. These are sometimes referred to as looked after children (LAC). These are children and young people who are in the care of the local authority, have been adopted or fostered, or are in the care of relatives.

Clerk
A specifically trained administrator who is there to advise the governors but is not a governor.

CME
Children missing education. If a child/student fails to attend school for ten days or more, or is not on any school roll and is not being home educated, then they are classed as a child missing education.

CoG
Chair of governors. This person is the member of the board/committee responsible for leading the governing board and working closely with the headteacher, head of school and senior leadership team.

Code of conduct
A set of rules around behaviour for the governors to follow as they undertake their roles in school.

Committee
A group of governors who work together for a specific function such as looking at personal development across the school by a whole governing body; consists of members drawn from the full governor group.

Conflict of interest
A situation in which a governor is in a position to derive personal benefit from actions or decisions made in their official capacity as a school governor. This must be declared and, if appropriate, the governor in question would withdraw from the decision-making process associated with this aspect of the work.

CSE
Child sexual exploitation. A form of sexual abuse in which a child or young person is sexually exploited for money, power or status. This comes under the safeguarding agenda.

Department for Education (DfE)
A ministerial department supported by agencies and public bodies, which is responsible for children's services and education

including further and higher education policy, apprenticeships and wider skills in England.

Director
A member of the board of people that manages or oversees the affairs of an academy or MAT.

DSG
Dedicated schools grant. This is government funding for local authorities to fund schools that they manage; it does not include academies.

DSL
Designated safeguarding lead. This is the person in school who is responsible for the safeguarding of children and young people at all levels. In large schools, there are likely to be several people undertaking this role.

ECT
Early career teacher. This replaces the previously used term 'newly qualified teacher' (NQT). This is a teacher in their first two years of teaching, who will have a reduced timetable and further regular training after their initial teacher training.

EHCP
Education and healthcare plan. This is for children and young people up to the age of 25 years who require more support than is available through the special educational needs support. EHCPs identify educational, health and social needs and strategies to meet those individual needs.

EHE
Elective home education. This is where children and young people are educated by their parents at home.

Evidence
Facts and information on which to base judgements about developments in school.

Exclusion
The process of removing a child/student from school as a result of serious behaviour.

Executive head
An executive head has no substantive headship in any school but is the strategic leader of more than one school, a federation or a collaboration of schools.

Ex-officio
A person who is automatically a governor or able to attend meetings of a governing body by virtue of the office they usually hold – for example, the headteacher and/or executive head.

Extraordinary general meeting
An extraordinary general meeting is arranged outside the planned and agreed dates for meetings, usually to discuss a specific and urgent matter.

EYFS
Early Years Foundation Stage. This outlines the standards for the learning, development and care of children from birth to five years. All schools and Ofsted-registered early years providers must follow the EYFS requirements, including childminders, preschools, nurseries and reception classes in school.

Funding agreement
The agreed funding arrangements for schools. For those under the LEA, funding comes from the government to the LEA for dispersal. For academies, it comes directly from the Department for Education.

GAG
Stands for general academies grant and is paid to the academy trust by the Secretary of State towards the normal running costs or capital expenditure of each academy.

GCSE
General Certificate of Secondary Education. The examinations taken by students in Year 11 (15–16-year-olds) nationally. Graded from 1–9 where 9 is the highest level awarded.

Headteacher
The most senior leader in the school, who is responsible for all the children/students and staff.

HMI
His Majesty's Inspectors. Appointed as inspectors of schools, nurseries, colleges and teacher training providers.

Instrument of government
For LEA-maintained schools, this is the document that records the name of the school and the constitution of its governing body. The governing board prepares the draft instrument of government and submits it to the local authority to consider whether it complies with the relevant legal requirements. The local authority must supply a copy of the instrument of government to each member of the governing board under the *School Governance (Constitution) (England) Regulation 2012* (UK Government, 2012).

ITT
Initial teacher training. This can be completed for primary years as part of a three-year undergraduate degree, a postgraduate year of study or one year in school (School Direct, School Centred Initial Teacher Training [SCITT] or an apprenticeship) or Teach First. For secondary teachers, the process is only through a postgraduate year of study or one year in school (School Direct, SCITT or an apprenticeship) or Teach First. Once the training period has been completed, teachers are deemed to have achieved qualified teacher status (QTS). This is also sometimes referred to as initial teacher education (ITE).

KS
Key stage. The blocking of specific years of study across the school years:

KS 1 – Years 1 and 2
KS 2 – Years 3, 4, 5 and 6
KS 3 – Years 7, 8 and 9
KS 4 – Years 10 and 11
KS 5 – Years 12 and 13.

LAC
Looked after children; sometimes referred to as children looked after (CLA). These are children and young people who are in the care of the local authority, who have been adopted or fostered, or who are in the care of relatives.

LADO
Local authority designated officer. The person who should be notified when it has been alleged that someone who works with children has:

- behaved in a way which has harmed or might harm a child;
- possibly committed a criminal offence against a child.

Learning walk
A short and informal visit to a classroom, in which senior teachers and/or subject leads focus and observe any specific area of education and then offer detailed feedback to those observed. This is sometimes used for the process when governors visit schools to look at specific areas of the curriculum and/or school development.

LEA
Local Education Authority. The body that oversees the educational provision of school places, children/students with SEND and children/students who have been excluded from schools.

Link governor
A member of the governing body who is linked to a specific class, subject or other responsibility.

Local governing board
Another term used for local governing bodies and often used interchangeably, although this can be the term used for the trustees governing a MAT.

Local governing body
A group of governors who are delegated responsibility for the oversight of particular areas of the school's function that depend upon the scheme of delegation within a MAT.

MASH
Multi-agency safeguarding hub. This is a partnership between the police, health, councils and other key partner agencies working together to safeguard children, young people and adults.

MAT
Multi-academy trust. A group of academies that come together to form a charitable company, which runs all the schools in the trust.

Minutes
A record of the meetings held. Minutes should be an accurate reflection of the content of the discussions and indicate decisions made.

NC
National Curriculum. This sets out the programmes of study and attainment targets for all subjects at all four key stages of compulsory education, from 5–18 years of age. All local authority-maintained schools in England must teach these programmes of study.

NEETS
The term used for school leavers who are not in education, employment or training.

NLE
National leaders of education. These are outstanding headteachers who work with other schools in challenging circumstances to support improvements.

NLG
National leaders of governance. These are highly effective and experienced chairs of governors who support chairs of governors in other schools.

Ofsted
The Office for Standards in Education, Children's Services and Skills. Members of Ofsted inspect and regulate services that care for children and young people, and services providing education and skills for learners of all ages.

Panel
A small group of governors brought together for a specific purpose – for example, exclusions or complaints.

POT
Position of trust. The term used to refer to people who work with children and young people, in either a paid or voluntary capacity.

QTS
Qualified teacher status. This is required in England and Wales to work as a teacher in most schools under local authority control. It indicates these people have been trained and recommended for the status.

Quorum
The minimum number of governors required for a meeting to go ahead.

Recruitment
The process of advertising and selecting a candidate for a post in school, whether a teacher, teaching assistant or administrator.

Register of interests
The register of any interests that governors and others working in the school have that could influence their decision-making. This is updated annually unless circumstances change during the year, in which case it is the responsibility of the governor or member of staff to notify the clerk.

SACRE
Standing Advisory Council for Religious Education. This is a statutory body that advises the local authority on matters relating to religious education including collective worship and the religious education curriculum.

Safeguarding
The process of keeping all children, young people and vulnerable adults safe from harm.

SATs
These are the end of key stage assessments (Statutory assessment tasks) in Years 2 and 6 (7 and 11 years of age). They are optional at KS 1 from 2023.

Scheme of delegation
A reference document showing what authority the trust has delegated to committees under the powers of its governing document.

School development/improvement plan
The document that sets out the areas for development/improvement during the current academic year. Includes information about milestones, success criteria, who is responsible for leading each area and how it is to be monitored.

School performance data
The data collected on every school in relation to exam and test results, Ofsted reports and financial information.

Section 48 inspections
If a school is designated as having a religious character, then the denominational education and collective worship will be inspected under section 48 of the *Education Act 2005* (UK Government, 2005). These are conducted in addition to Ofsted inspections.

Self-evaluation
The process of examining the previous year's performance across the school and completing a self-evaluation form (SEF) before compiling a new school improvement/development plan.

SEMH
Social, emotional and mental health needs. A type of SEND where children and young people have severe difficulty in managing their emotions and/or behaviour.

SENCo
Special educational needs co-ordinator. A member of teaching staff who has received specific additional training within the first two years of their role and is responsible for the day-to-day operation of the school's SEND policy.

SEND
Special educational needs and disability, for children and young people who have a difficulty or disability that makes learning harder for them in comparison with others of their age.

SIAMS
The Statutory Inspection of Anglican and Methodist Schools is the Church of England and Methodist Church's outworking of the requirements of section 48 of the *Education Act 2005* (UK Government, 2005).

Stakeholder
A party or person affected by a school or who has an effect on the school – for example, children, students, parents, local planners.

Standing orders
A prescribed procedure that is often associated with formal meetings, such as the number of people required for a meeting to go ahead – a quorum.

Studio schools
Small free schools (usually with around 300 pupils) teaching mainstream qualifications through project-based learning. This means working in realistic situations as well as learning academic subjects. Students work with local employers and a personal coach, and follow a curriculum designed to give them the skills and qualifications they need in work, or to take up further education.

Suspensions
This is the term used for children/students who have been excluded from school for a short period of full days or part of days, such as during lunchtimes.

Teach First
A specific salaried route into teaching intended to target the most deprived areas of the country and a programme where candidates are expected to give two years to teaching. Candidates must be graduates and can apply to teach secondary, primary or early years levels.

Terms of reference
Set out the scope and limitations of governing bodies and/or committees.

Trust member
A member of the trust board for a MAT.

UTC
University technical college. A specific type of academy sponsored by universities, further education colleges or employers, usually taking pupils aged 14–18 years.

Vice chair
A member of the board of governors who deputises for the chair whenever and wherever necessary.

References

UK Government (2005) *Education Act 2005*. [online] Available at: www.legislation.gov.uk/ukpga/2005/18/contents (accessed 5 December 2022).

UK Government (2012) *The School Governance (Constitution) (England) Regulation 2012*. [online] Available at: www.legislation.gov.uk/uksi/2012/1034/contents/made (accessed 4 December 2022).

INDEX

Note: page numbers in **bold** denote tables.

academies, 125–8, 160
academisation, 131
accountability, 36, 98, 101, 125
agenda, for meeting, 83–91
alternative provision (AP), 125
associate roles, 40
Association of Muslim Schools (AMS) UK, 147
attendance, and safeguarding, **58**

behaviour management, and safeguarding, **58**
benchmarking, 117
Blair, Tony, 131

care quality commission (CQC), 125
case studies
    clerk, 50
    foundation governors, 39
    governor's meeting, 94–5
    headteachers, 25–6
    inspections, 145, 153

local authority governors, 37
local authority support and training, 159
motives for becoming governors, 5–6
non-teaching governors, 29
parent governors, 34
safeguarding governors, 62
school visits, 111
self-evaluation form, 118
services to schools, 130
subcommittees, 97–8
suspension and exclusion, 73
teachers as governors, 27–8
Catholic schools, 6, 68, 148, **149**
chair, 45–51
    board/committee business meetings, 49–51
    governance, 46–7
    improvement plan, 49

chair (*continued*)
- leadership and governing team development, 47–8
- and senior leadership team, 48

Children and Families Act 2014, 125

children who are looked after (CLA), safeguarding, **61**

children/students, talking to, 121–3

Christian schools, inspection of, 153–4
- Catholic schools, 148, **149**
- Church of England schools, 150–1
- Greek Orthodox schools, 152
- Methodist schools, 150

Church of England, 45

Church of England schools, 39, 69, 150

clerks, 30–2

Code of Conduct, 7, 17
- breach of, 12
- commitments, 8–10
- communications, 9–11
- confidentiality, 9
- conflicts of interest, 11–12
- relationships, 9
- role and responsibilities, 8

commitments, 8–10

communications, 9–11

community/co-opted governors, 35–7

complaints and appeals, 71–2

compliance, 36

composition of governing bodies, 6

Confederation of School Trusts, **161**

confidentiality, 9, 17

conflicts of interest, 11–12

councillor, 37

curriculum, and safeguarding, **58**

data exploration, 111–14

Department for Education (DfE), 22, 72, 123–4
- Governance Handbook, 4
- information, 157

Designated Safeguarding Lead (DSL), 53

Diocesan Board of Education, 69

directors, 41–3

diversity, 36

INDEX 181

Educare, **162**
Education Act 2005, 133
    section 48, 39, 40, 69, 133, 147–54
    Christian schools under, 147
    Hindu schools under, 153
    Jewish schools under, 152–3
    Muslim schools under, 147
    Seventh Day Adventist schools under, 152
    Sikh schools under, 153
Education and Skills Funding Agency, 129
effective governance, 4–5
emails, 9–11
equality, 36
e-safety
    governors, 66–7
    and safeguarding, **61**
executive headteachers, 22–3
external governors, 33, 43
    associate roles, 40
    community/co-opted governors, 35–7
    foundation governors, 38–40
    local authority governors, 37–8
    parent governors, 33–5
    partnership governors, 40–1
    trustees, members and directors, 41–3

faith schools, 6, 39, 68
finances, 18
foundation governors, 38–40, 45, 68–70
free schools, 129–30

governance
    definition of, 3–4
    effectiveness of, 4–5
    information sources, 160–2
Governor Hub, **162**
governor panels, 71–5
    complaints and appeals, 71–2
    pay committees, 75
    suspensions and exclusions, 72–5
governors
    attendance of, 9
    motives for becoming, 16–19
    process of becoming, 7
    terms of office, 5–6

Governors for Schools, **161**
governors' meetings, 83–96, 100
    agenda for, 83–91
    preparation for, 93–6
    roles within, 92–3
Governors' Virtual Office, **162**
Greek Orthodox schools, inspection of, 152

heads of school, 23, 26–7
headteachers, 23–6
Hindu schools, inspection of, 153

inclusion, 36
induction, and safeguarding, **58**
inspections, 133–54
    under *Education Act 2005* see *Education Act 2005*, section 48
    Ofsted inspections *see* Ofsted inspections
    sample questions, **138**
    summary of, **135**
Inspiring Governance, **161**
interrelationships, 36

Jewish schools, inspection of, 152–3

Keeping Children Safe in Education (KCSIE), 9, 53
Krishna Avanti Trust, 153

link governors, 70
local authority, support and training from, 158
local authority governors, 37–8
Local Education Authority (LEA), 124–5

maintained schools, 21–2
MATs/trust, support and training from, 160
members, 41–3
Methodist schools, inspection of, 250
monitoring, 101–23
    children/students, talking to, 121–2
    data exploration, 111–14
    reports analysis and presentations, 114–15
    school development plan/improvement plan (SDP/SIP), 115–19
    school tours, 101–2
    school visits, 102–11
    teachers, discussion with, 119–20

multi academy trusts (MATs), 21, 22, 128–9

Muslim schools, inspection of, 147

National and Regional Schools Commissioners, 128

National Governance Association (NGA), 3, 7, **161**

Network of Sikh Organisations, 153

Nolan Principles, 13–16

non-teaching governors, 28–9

Ofsted inspections, 39, 115, 125, 133, 134–46, 147

on call arrangements, safeguarding, **61**

parent governors, 33–5

parish councillor, 38

partnership governors, 40–1

pay committees, 75

Pikuach, 152–3

policies, and safeguarding, **58**

Pupil Premium Grant (PPG), 65–6, 113

recruitment of staff, 76–80

reflective supervision, and safeguarding, **58**

regulations, 6

relationships, 9

reports, analysis and presentations of, 114–15

roles and responsibilities, 45, 80

    of chair *see* chair

    complaints and appeals, 71–2

    of e-safety governors, 66–7

    of foundation governors, 68–70

    of governing body, 8

    of link governors, 70

    meeting related, 92–3

    and monitoring *see* monitoring

    pay committees, 75

    of safeguarding governors *see* safeguarding governors

    of SEND governors, 63–4

    suspensions and exclusions, 72–5

    of vice-chairs, 52–62

    of well-being governors, 67–8

safeguarding, 9, **61**

safeguarding governors, 52–62

    and physical environment, 53–4

safeguarding governors (*continued*)
    safeguarding agenda, areas linked to, 57
    safer recruitment, 54, **58**
    single central register (SCR), 54–7
    training for, 53
School Complaints Unit (SCU), 71
school development plan/improvement plan (SDP/SIP), 115–19
school governors, 21–2, 31–2
    and clerks, 30–2
    executive heads, 22–3
    heads of school, 26–7
    headteachers, 23–6
    non-teaching governors, 28–9
    teachers, 27–8
School Staffing (England) Regulations (2009), 54
school tours, 101–2
school trips, safeguarding, **61**
school visits, 102–11
    additional events, 110–11
    guidance after, 109
    guidance during, 108
    preparation for, 102–8
secondary school report, 23–4
Secretary of State for Education, 71
section 48 inspections *see Education Act 2005*, section 48
self-evaluation, 36
self-evaluation form (SEF), 117
SEND governors, **61**, 63–4
services to schools, 130–1
Seven Principles of Public Life, 13–16
Seventh Day Adventist schools, inspection of, 152
Sikh schools, inspection of, 153
single central register (SCR), 54–7
skills audit, 35–6
staff recruitment, 76–80
Statutory Inspection of Anglican and Methodist Schools (SIAMS), 69, 150, 151
strategy, 36
studio schools, 129
subcommittees, 96–100
    curriculum and standards, 96–8
    guiding principles, 97
    terms of reference, 97–8
subject leader questions, 119, **120**

support and training, 18, 162–3
suspensions and exclusions, 72–5

teachers
    discussion with, 119–20
    as governors, 27–8
teamwork, 36
terms of office, 5–6
terms of reference, 97–8, 176
Timpson Report, 74
training, and safeguarding, **58**
transitions, safeguarding, **61**

Trust Deed, 69
trustees, 41–3

university technical college (UTC), 129

vice-chairs, 52–62

well-being governors, **61**, 67–8
work-based governor groups, 160
working relationship, effective, 25–6